Everlasting Life

by
Mrs. Oliver B. Greene

The Gospel Hour, Inc., Oliver B. Greene, Director
Box 2024, Greenville, South Carolina 29602

First printing, July 1973—50,000 copies
Second printing, September, 1973—50,000 copies
Third printing, November 1973—25,000 copies

$5.00

Foreword

There is much confusion among Christians concerning the subject dealt with in this book. No doubt this is the most controversial subject there is in the churches today. The confusion that exists is due largely to the use of denominational terms by ministers and teachers. I have never used denominational terms in my sermons or my books; I use *Bible* terms, such as the name of this book: *EVERLASTING LIFE.* I believe in everlasting (or eternal) life for the following reasons:

1. The Word of God tells me that God so loved the world that He gave His only begotten Son to die for the poor lost sinner (John 3:16, 17). Jesus, God's only begotten Son, came into the world and died for sinners (Matt. 20:28; John 10:17, 18; Rom. 5:8).

2. Jesus is the One who saves the sinner; Jesus GIVES everlasting life to all who *believe ON* Him (John 3:36; 10:28) and COME to Him (Matt. 11:28; John 6:37). Eternal life is THE GIFT OF GOD through Jesus His Son (Rom. 6:23).

3. Jesus is "THE AUTHOR AND FINISHER OF OUR FAITH" (Heb. 12:2). He is also "the Author of ETERNAL SALVATION" (Heb. 5:9).

4. Jesus is not only the Author and the Finisher of our faith, the Author of eternal salvation—HE IS OUR SALVATION: "... *Christ IN YOU,* the hope of glory" (Col. 1:27).

5. God saves us through the finished work of Jesus—His life, death, burial, resurrection, and ascension—BUT, *God saves us FOR JESUS' SAKE* (Eph. 4:32; I John 2:12).

6. Since God SAVES US, and since salvation is JESUS WITHIN US (Col. 1:27), and since we are SEALED BY THE HOLY SPIRIT until the day of redemption (Eph. 4:30), we are SAVED WITH THE PERFECT SALVATION provided by THE PERFECT GOD through HIS PERFECT SON—and we are SEALED with THE PERFECT SEAL, the Third Person of the Holy Trinity. Since God is PERFECT, God could not provide an IMPERFECT SALVATION! God COULD NOT provide an *inferior redemption* that might spoil or decay if man did not add his righteous living day by day to keep God's redemption from deteriorating. If the believer fails to live as a believer should, he will lose his reward (I Cor. 3:12-15); but the redemption, the salvation from sin, the eternal life within us is GOD'S—"not of WORKS, lest any man should boast" (Eph. 2:9).

7. ALL THAT GOD HAS EVER DONE IS RIGHT, RIGHTEOUS, AND ETERNAL: "I know that, *whatsoever God doeth, it shall be for ever:* nothing can be put to it, nor any thing taken from

4

it: and God doeth it, that men should fear before Him" (Eccl. 3:14). THIS IS NOT FATALISM; *this is FAITH*—and eternal life is ours BY FAITH!

8. I believe in EVERLASTING LIFE because I believe Romans 8:28-39. Since I believe these precious verses, I believe when one is saved, born again, cleansed by the blood of Jesus, *that person is a possessor of ETERNAL LIFE* and "shall NEVER PERISH" (John 10:28). NOTHING—"neither death, nor life, . . . *nor any other creature"*— CAN, or WILL, separate that child of God from the LOVE OF GOD!

9. One born again is a possessor of DIVINE NATURE (II Pet. 1:4), a possessor of the Holy Spirit (John 3:5; Rom. 8:9). He is *led* by the Holy Spirit (Rom. 8:14); he is *sealed* by the Holy Spirit (Eph. 4:30); he is a NEW CREATURE (II Cor. 5:17), God's son NOW (I John 3:1-3). He is HID WITH CHRIST IN GOD (Col. 3:3). One born of God has within His heart *the GRACE of God.* God's grace *saved* us (Eph. 2:8)—BUT GRACE DOES NOT STOP THERE:

"For *the grace of God that bringeth salvation* hath appeared to all men, *TEACHING us that, denying ungodliness and worldly lusts, we should live soberly, righteously, and godly, in this present world;* looking for that blessed hope, and the glorious appearing of the great God and our Saviour Jesus Christ; who gave Himself for us, that He might redeem us from all iniquity, and purify unto Himself a peculiar people, zealous of good works" (Titus 2:11-14).

The Apostle Paul—to whom God revealed the mystery of the New Testament Church, the mystery of Jew and Gentile together in ONE BODY IN CHRIST (Eph. 3:1-12; Col. 1:27)—*assures believers* in these words: "*. . . for I know WHOM* (note, not WHAT, but WHOM—Jesus) *I have believed, and am PERSUADED that He is ABLE TO KEEP that which I have COMMITTED UNTO HIM against THAT DAY*" (II Tim. 1:12).

And—"BEING CONFIDENT OF THIS VERY THING, that HE which hath begun a good work in you WILL PERFORM IT UNTIL THE DAY OF JESUS CHRIST" (Phil. 1:6).

Eternal life begins through faith in the finished work of Jesus; and eternal life *continues* by faith in *His* (NOT OUR) *ability, His strength!* (Rom. 1:17). Final victory over the world, the flesh, and the devil is FAITH IN JESUS (I John 5:4,5). Remember—Jesus is the AUTHOR and He is the FINISHER of our FAITH (Heb. 12:2).

One reason for the controversy among Christians concerning eternal life, is that some believe all church members are saved; but *this is not true!* One who loves the world and the things of the world, one who loves pleasure more than he loves God, *has NEVER BEEN SAVED* (I John 2:15-17; II Tim. 3:4). Such a person may be a good church member, but HE IS NOT SAVED! The truth is,

6

in *most* churches there are more members *lost* than *saved.* "By their fruits ye shall know them" (Matt. 7:20)—and a church member who *continually* bears the fruits of the world and the flesh—IS NOT SAVED! The fruits of a *Christian* are "love, joy, peace, longsuffering, gentleness, goodness, faith, meekness, temperance" (Gal. 5:22, 23).

Joining the church does not save a sinner; being a good church member does not save; becoming a Sunday school teacher does not save; becoming a minister does not save. There are many *unsaved* church members, Sunday school teachers, preachers, evangelists—and even some missionaries (Matt. 7:21-23; II Cor. 11:13-15). *Man* looks on the outward appearance—but *GOD looks on the HEART* (I Sam. 16:7).

ETERNAL LIFE is the GIFT of God! (Eph. 2:8; Rom. 6:23). REWARD in heaven will be determined by our WORKS (I Cor. 3:11-15).

If you have eternal life, YOU KNOW IT! You are SURE that you have eternal life—BUT YOU CANNOT BE SURE ABOUT ANYONE ELSE BUT YOURSELF! You see fruits of salvation in many lives, but you cannot KNOW FOR SURE that any person except YOURSELF is TRULY BORN AGAIN!

FOR THIRTY-NINE YEARS I have put the promises in God's Word to the test; they are ALL true! I have had no desire to return to the life of sin; there is nothing there for me—NOR FOR

ANY CHILD OF GOD! *I believe* the TRUTH
set forth in this book!
—*Evangelist Oliver B. Greene*

Everlasting Life

"For God so loved the world, that He gave His only begotten Son, that whosoever believeth in Him should not perish, but have everlasting life" (John 3:16).

Can a believer lose his salvation?

This is one of the most controversial issues among Christian people today. It is not my intention to argue this doctrinal question or take up banners for either side. But because there is so much misunderstanding on this subject I want us to examine the Scriptures, forget denominational church doctrine, and find out, according to God's Word, what to believe and what to stand on.

In churches today we find *two distinctly different groups,* and the attitude of either group causes harm to the very souls they are trying to help. The first of these groups we might classify as the "hard-headed" fanatical crowd who preach and argue "once saved, always saved." These people are so involved in their *doctrine* that they often neglect to examine their own souls to see if they have been *truly born again*—or if they have been deceived by their doctrine and by church

9

membership. So determined are they to defend their doctrinal position that they fail to see that many church members are not saved but have only "joined the church"—perhaps when they were children—without understanding God's plan of salvation and being born again.

Furthermore, if God convicts some of these unsaved church members and they desire to *be* saved, the fanatics on the subject of "once saved, always saved" are on hand to argue their doctrine. In our own ministry we have had people come to the altar seeking salvation, admitting that they only *"thought"* they had been saved previously. And I have heard personal workers argue with these dear people, telling them that they did not *need* to be *saved,* but only to be renewed into fellowship with Christ. What terrible stumbling blocks such personal workers are! Instead of permitting (or helping) the individual to accept Christ, they take the opportunity to expound their doctrine of "Eternal Security," thus turning the footsteps of a repentant sinner away from the cross of Calvary.

If a person tells me that he has never been saved I dare not question or argue. I believe him because only he and God know whether he is saved or lost. I may *think* a person is saved, but I cannot *know for sure* whether or not he is saved. It is true that the devil has deceived thousands of people into thinking they are secure just because they joined a church and were baptized, but once a person is truly born into the family of God *he KNOWS it!*

There is *a second group* which stands on the opposite extreme concerning the question of whether or not a believer can lose his salvation. This second group is composed of people who are so opposed to the term "eternal security" that they will not help a true *backslider* to come back to God, but will insist that he has lost his salvation because he has sinned, and therefore needs to be *saved again.* Such fanaticism keeps many Christians confused, never sure whether they are lost or saved. They live in fear and uncertainty, worth nothing to the church or to God insofar as service is concerned.

Which of these two groups is worse? I see potential danger in both of them, danger of letting souls die and go to hell. Both groups are interested in defending a doctrine, not in helping souls in need. Both groups will have to give an account to God at the Judgment—and woe unto those who have stood in the way of sinners who needed to be saved, those who have hindered backsliders who needed to come back to God, and those who have kept Christians confused and uncertain of their salvation, thus rendering them unfruitful and of little or no service as soul winners.

The answer to the question "Can a believer lose his salvation?" or, "Do you believe in Eternal

Security?'' involves more than a simple "Yes" or "No." With the answer there must be a foundation, an explanation, or we will only succeed in confusing people more than ever. There are Scriptures which can be used on this subject, pro and con, but as a starting point I want us to look at Romans 8:28-39:

"And we know that all things work together for good to them that love God, to them who are the called according to His purpose. For whom He did foreknow, He also did predestinate to be conformed to the image of His Son, that He might be the firstborn among many brethren. Moreover whom He did predestinate, them He also called: and whom He called, them He also justified: and whom He justified, them He also glorified.

"What shall we then say to these things? If God be for us, who can be against us? He that spared not His own Son, but delivered Him up for us all, how shall He not with Him also freely give us all things? Who shall lay anything to the charge of God's elect? It is God that justifieth. Who is he that condemneth? It is Christ that died, yea rather, that is risen again, who is even at the right hand of God, who also maketh intercession for us.

"Who shall separate us from the love of Christ? Shall tribulation, or distress, or persecution, or famine, or nakedness, or peril, or sword? As it is written, For thy sake we are killed all the day long; we are accounted as sheep for the slaughter.

"Nay, in all these things we are more than conquerors through Him that loved us. *For I am persuaded, that neither death, nor life, nor angels, nor principalities, nor powers, nor things present, nor things to come, nor height, nor depth, NOR ANY OTHER CREATURE, shall be able to separate us from the love of God, which is in Christ Jesus our Lord."*

Verse 35 of this passage asks the question, *"Who shall separate us from the love of Christ?"* In other words, after we have been truly born again, justified by faith (v. 33) and become Christians in the true sense of the word, after our names have been written in the Lamb's Book of Life (Rev. 21:27), *who (or what) can separate us from Christ?* Verses 38 and 39 of our present passage give a direct, God-inspired answer to this question, complete and clear:

"Neither death, nor life" shall separate us from the love of Christ. Nothing in *life* and nothing in *death*—or *after* death—can separate us from Christ.

". . . nor angels, nor principalities, nor powers" can separate us from Christ. When Christ rose from the grave *He "spoiled principalities and powers,* He made a shew of them openly" (Col. 2:15). The Bible makes clear the truth that the Lord Jesus Christ conquered death, hell, and the grave. He defeated Satan and his emissaries. In

Revelation 1:18 the risen, glorified Christ declared: "I am He that liveth, and was dead; and, behold, I am alive for evermore, Amen; and have the keys of hell and of death!"

How comforting it is to know that Satan is a defeated foe! This is a Bible fact, not a "maybe so" or "hope so." His defeat was accomplished by the perfect death of a perfect Saviour, and that defeat was confirmed by our Lord's resurrection and ascension to the right hand of the Father on high (I Cor. 15:20; Heb. 1:3). Christ finished the work He came into the world to do. He defeated Satan, death, and hell; therefore no part of the satanic force can separate us from Christ.

". . . nor things present, nor things to come" can separate us from the love of Christ—and just in case this might not cover everything, the Apostle Paul added, under inspiration, *"nor height, nor depth, NOR ANY OTHER CREATURE"* can separate us "from the love of God, which is in Christ Jesus, our Lord."

This Scripture plainly teaches that the believer is safe, *very* safe—but this promise is *only* for the *believer*. There is an "IF" involved here—IF one has been born again. Upon that one little word hangs the promise, and the "if" has caused many people to become confused. You see, Romans 8:28-39 applies only to those who are *born again*— not to all who have joined the church. It does not apply to those who "think" they are saved, nor

14

to those whom *we* think are saved, *but to those who ARE saved.*

Eternal Life — What Does It Mean?

"And this is the record, that God hath given to us eternal life, and this life is in His Son" (I John 5:11).

When we speak of eternal life—or *everlasting* life—we mean that a poor, lost sinner has accepted Jesus Christ as Saviour, has received a new nature, and has become a new creation in Christ. "... old things are passed away; behold, ALL things are become *new*" (II Cor. 5:17). The born again believer has been made partaker of divine nature (II Pet. 1:4). Give thought to the wonder of this statement—the almost incomprehensible wonder that a poor, lost, wretched sinner can be so loved of God that his sins are forgiven, he is justified before the throne of God, and he is made *partaker of the DIVINE NATURE of God.*

This does not happen to one who only *professes* to be saved, who joins a church and offers "lip service" to the Lord Jesus Christ by saying that he has been saved. In this world today, from east to west, from north to south, people—especially *young* people—are participating in "religion"; but that does not necessarily mean that they are saved, that they have become partakers of divine nature and recipients of eternal life.

Jesus Himself brought out this fact in Matthew

7:21-23 when He declared, "Not every one that saith unto me, Lord, Lord, shall enter into the Kingdom of Heaven; but he that doeth the will of my Father which is in heaven. Many will say to me in that day, Lord, Lord, have we not prophesied in thy name? and in thy name have cast out devils? and in thy name done many wonderful works? And then will I profess unto them, *I NEVER knew you:* depart from me, ye that work iniquity."

Notice Jesus will not say to these people, "I once knew you. . . . You once had eternal life." No, He will say, "I *NEVER* knew you!" This is the same crowd of whom Jesus said, in Matthew 15:8, "This people draweth nigh unto me with their mouth, and honoureth me with their lips; but their heart is far from me."

So it will not be everyone who says "Lord, Lord" who will enter into the Kingdom of Heaven, but those who do the will of God—and John's Gospel tells us plainly what the will of God is. In John 6:40 Jesus said, "This is the will of Him that sent me, that every one which seeth the Son, and believeth on Him, may have everlasting life: and I will raise him up at the last day." God's will is that we believe on His Son for everlasting life.

Those Whom Jesus Knows

In John 10:27, 28 Jesus declared, "My sheep hear my voice, and *I know them*, and they follow me: and I give unto them eternal life; and they shall never perish, neither shall any man pluck them out of my hand."

How definite, concise, and clear! Of one group— the born again children of God—Jesus says, "I KNOW them." Of the other group—"professors" of religion but not "possessors" of eternal life—He says, *"I NEVER KNEW YOU."* There would be no controversial issue, no questions asked about eternal life, if everyone recognized the fact that these two groups exist—one saved, one lost. Many times the "wheat" and the "tares" are so mixed that only time and eternity will reveal their true classification (Matt. 13:24-30).

The question is often asked, "Suppose a man professes to be saved, joins the church, teaches a Sunday school class and performs many other religious works. He later turns back into the world, and by his life denies the Lord and the Gospel he once professed. What happens to that man when he dies? Is he saved? Or is he lost?"

This hypothetical question is answered for us in God's Word. In I John 2:19 the beloved disciple said of such people, "They went out from us, but *they were not OF us;* for if they had been of us, they would no doubt have *continued with us:* but they went out, *that they might be made manifest* that they were not all of us."

This Scripture plainly shows that it is possible to join a church, work faithfully in that church—

17

perhaps even serve as a deacon or Sunday school teacher, join in many religious endeavors—and yet be unsaved. Yes, an unsaved person can—and often does—work in a church, and he (or she, as the case may be) can produce good results. Bear in mind that it is THE WORD which is used of God; and the Word, even though given forth by an unsaved person, can accomplish great things. We are *saved* by the Word, "being born again, not of corruptible seed, but of incorruptible, *by THE WORD OF GOD, which liveth and abideth for ever"* (I Pet. 1:23).

It is true that God can use the Word to produce greater works when it is proclaimed by a consecrated, born again believer than when it is proclaimed by a person who merely *professes* Christianity. But God has promised that His Word shall not return unto Him void, that it shall accomplish that which He pleases and shall prosper in that whereto He sends it (Isa. 55:11). Therefore it cannot be denied that He *uses* the Word regardless of who sends it forth.

Jesus Is Eternal Life

I am often asked, "Do you believe in 'Eternal Security'?" Or, "Do you believe 'once saved, always saved'?" *I believe what the Bible teaches. I believe in ETERNAL LIFE,* and eternal life is Jesus Christ our Saviour:

"This is the record, that God hath given to us

eternal life, and this life is in His Son. He that hath the Son *hath life;* and he that hath not the Son of God *hath not LIFE....* This is the true God, and eternal life" (I John 5:11, 12, 20).

"For the life was manifested, and we have seen it, and bear witness, and shew unto you *that eternal life, which was with the Father, and was manifested unto us"* (I John 1:2).

Jesus is our eternal life because of His one perfect sacrifice on the cross: "This Man, after He had offered *one sacrifice for sins FOR EVER,* sat down on the right hand of God; . . . for by *ONE offering* He hath perfected for ever them that are sanctified" (Heb. 10:12, 14).

Throughout the Book of Hebrews we see contrasted the *many* sacrifices offered by the priests in the *Old* Testament and the *one perfect sacrifice* of Christ on Calvary's cross. Under Old Testament law, every time an Israelite sinned he needed to offer a sacrifice: "And every priest standeth daily ministering and offering oftentimes the *same sacrifices,* which can never take away sins" (Heb. 10:11). The same sacrifice, many times for the same sins, day after day, year after year. Then, once a year, on the Day of Atonement, the entire Israelite nation had to sacrifice a new offering to God. Why? Because "it is not possible that the blood of bulls and of goats should *take away* sins" (Heb. 10:4). But verse 14 of this tenth chapter of Hebrews tells us that by His one offering, His one sacrifice, Christ *"hath perfected FOR EVER* them that are sanctified."

Notice this verse does not tell us that Christ has perfected them that are sanctified "for as long as they are *faithful,"* but *"FOR EVER."* The "for ever" depends upon Christ and His atonement for sin, not upon us, our works, or our faithfulness. Those who place a *condition* on eternal life are insulting the finished work of Christ. Of course they do not mean to do so, but their interpretation of eternal life reduces Christ's sacrificial death to the level of the sacrifices of bulls and goats, sacrifices which were made under the Law and had to be repeated—over and over and over again.

Is the Assurance of Salvation Dangerous?

Those who would thus limit the efficacy of Christ's sacrifice of Himself are afraid of the *assurance* of eternal life, lest such assurance cause Christians to be careless in their Christian life. Therefore they hold great fear over the heads of Christians, declaring that eternal life is eternal *depending upon the faithfulness of each individual!* They teach that when a person is saved, all of his sins are forgiven *up to that moment*—and that he must keep his record clean from then on. If he fails (and he surely *will* fail) he will be lost again and must be saved all over again.

How can this be? It is certainly not in accordance with God's Word. Hebrews 7:26 and 27 speaks of Christ as "an High Priest . . . who is holy, harmless, undefiled, separate from sinners, and made higher than the heavens; who needeth not daily, as those (Old Testament) high priests, to offer up sacrifice, first for His own sins, and then for the people's: *for this He did ONCE,* when He offered up Himself."

Christ has "an *unchangeable* priesthood, wherefore He is able also to save them to the uttermost that come unto God by Him, seeing He ever liveth to make intercession for them" (Heb. 7:24, 25).

Someone may ask, "What about *future* sins? I know Christ died to save me, and I know He put all of my sins under the blood when I was saved. But what if I sin *after* I am saved?" May the Lord help you to see that when He died on the cross of Calvary He paid for those sins, too! If this is difficult to comprehend, ask yourself how many sins you had committed when Christ died. *NONE, of course, because you had not even been born.* The marvelous truth is that when Christ paid the sin-debt, *all* of your sins were yet future.

I Peter 2:24 tells us that Christ "His own self bare our sins in His own body on the tree, that we, being dead to sins, should live unto righteousness: by whose stripes ye were healed."

Isaiah prophesied of this before Christ was born. In Isaiah 53:5, 6 we read, "He was wounded for our transgressions, He was bruised for our iniquities: the chastisement of our peace was upon Him; and with His stripes we are healed. All we like sheep have gone astray; we have turned every one to his own way; and the Lord hath laid on Him *the iniquity of us ALL."*

Christ does not need to be crucified over and over again. God saw the sins of all the world from eternity to eternity, and He laid all of these sins upon His Son. Therefore the one sacrifice of the Lord Jesus Christ paid for all sins, past, present, and future. "For Christ also hath *once* suffered for sins, the Just for the unjust, that He might bring us to God, being put to death in the flesh, but quickened by the Spirit" (I Pet. 3:18).

When we accept Christ as Saviour, we are freed from the condemnation of sin—but that is not all. He has also made provision for the forgiveness of sins committed *after* we are saved. I John 1:9 assures us, "If we confess our sins, He is faithful and just to forgive us our sins, and to cleanse us from all unrighteousness." Then in Hebrews 9:24 we read, "For Christ is not entered into the holy places made with hands, which are the figures of the true; but *into heaven itself, now to appear in the presence of God FOR US."*

Does It Matter if a Christian Sins?

The scriptural assurance that eternal life *really IS ETERNAL* may give rise to the assumption that it does not matter if a Christian *does* sin.

Nothing could be further from the truth! The spiritual life of the believer is an entirely different subject, one upon which volumes could be written. As a matter of fact, volumes *have* been written on the responsibility, the reward, the chastisement, and the blessings of the true believer—and the subject is still not exhausted.

When a person trusts Christ as Saviour, that person has eternal life, he is born again, a new babe in Christ (I Pet. 2:2). The condemnation of sin is lifted from him (Rom. 8:1), but his duty as a child of God has just begun. It *does* matter, greatly, how a born again believer lives. If he sins, God deals with him as a disobedient child. He deals with him, not as a Judge, but as a Father: "For *whom the Lord loveth He chasteneth,* and scourgeth *every son* whom He receiveth. If ye endure chastening, God dealeth with you as with sons; for what son is he whom the father chasteneth not? But if ye be without chastisement, whereof all are partakers, then are ye bastards, and not sons.

"Furthermore we have had fathers of our flesh which corrected us, and we gave them reverence: shall we not *much rather* be in subjection unto *the Father of spirits,* and live? For they verily for a few days chastened us after their own pleasure; *but He for our profit, that we might be partakers of His holiness.* Now no chastening for the present seemeth to be joyous, but grievous; nevertheless afterward it yieldeth the peaceable fruit of right-eousness unto them which are exercised thereby" (Heb. 12:6-11).

The person who claims to be saved and yet thinks that it makes no difference how he lives *has never been truly saved.* I realize that this is a broad statement, but it is in accordance with God's Word. Proverbs 4:23 tells us that *out of the heart "are the issues of life."* Eternal life is Jesus Christ—"Christ in you, the hope of glory" (Col. 1:27). We who are born again are new crea-tions. Old things are passed away. All things have become new (II Cor. 5:17). The heart that once served sin now desires to serve God. Christ, in the Person of the Holy Spirit, dwells within the heart of the born again believer. Therefore I ask, *How can Christ deny Himself?* In other words, how can that which is *born AGAIN* (born from above) *desire* to sin?

The answer, of course, is that the born again believer *does not* want to sin. But bear in mind that there is a vast difference between *falling into temptation* and actually desiring to commit sin, sinning deliberately. A true Christian is led by the Spirit of God (Rom. 8:14), and the Holy Spirit of God will not lead a child of God to do that which is contrary to the will of God and contrary to God's Word. A true believer is not only *led* by the Spirit, he is also *sealed* by the Spirit until the day of redemption (Eph. 1:13, 14; 4:30). Therefore, being *indwelt* by the Spirit, *led* by the Spirit, and *sealed* by the Spirit, the born again believer will not have a *careless attitude* toward sin. His greatest desire will be to serve God.

Furthermore, if through weakness of the flesh the born again Christian yields to temptation and falls into sin, the convicting power of the Holy Spirit immediately convicts him of having done that which is not becoming to a child of God. Thus the Spirit shows the erring Christian that it *does* matter how he lives, and the believer who is out of fellowship with God is *miserably aware* that he has sinned and stands in need of forgiveness. Thank God for a redemption that provides not only freedom from the *penalty* of sin, but forgiveness for present and future sins! "If we walk in the light, as He is in the light, we have fellowship one with another, and the blood of Jesus Christ His Son cleanseth us from all sin" (I John 1:7).

God wants His children to live right more than they themselves want to. Jesus said to Peter, ". . . Satan hath desired to have you, that he may sift you as wheat: but *I have PRAYED for thee,* that thy faith fail not . . ." (Luke 22:31, 32). Jesus is just as concerned for us as He was for Peter, and He is ever watchful for us. We who are saved belong to Him. We are bought with a tremendous price. Our Saviour will not (as some teach) turn us over to Satan—nor will He allow a wayward child of God to "pluck himself" out of His hands! On the contrary, Philippians 1:6 assures us that "He which hath begun a good work in (us) will perform it until the day of Jesus Christ." Also in Hebrews 13:5 we read the precious promise, "He hath said, *I will never leave thee, nor forsake thee.*"

Many dear old saints of God who have been saved for thirty, forty, or fifty years will testify that they have had varied experiences in their Christian life. They declare that when they were wayward or willful—or simply negligent—the Holy Spirit never gave up, but brought them under the rod of God and eventually whipped them into subjection. But those saints were just as truly children of God while the whipping was being administered as when they were restored to joy and fellowship with the Lord.

A Present Possession

Eternal life is a NOW possession. We do not have to wait until we reach heaven to possess life eternal. True, we live in a body that will die; but even in our mortal bodies we possess eternal life. When Christ comes the second time, our bodies will be redeemed. *"Beloved, NOW are we the sons of God,* and it doth not yet appear what we shall be: but we know that, when He shall appear, *we shall be LIKE HIM;* for we shall see Him as He is"* (I John 3:2). Just as Jesus came the first time to redeem the soul, He will come again to redeem the body.

Adam's life was forfeited because of sin: "Wherefore, as by one man sin entered into the world, and death by sin; and so death passed upon all men, for that all have sinned. . . . But not as the offence, so also is the free gift. For if through the offence of one many be dead, much more the grace of God, and the gift by grace, which is by one Man, Jesus Christ, hath abounded unto many" (Rom. 5:12, 15).

ETERNAL life cannot be forfeited, because eternal life is Christ, and Christ (God in flesh) is eternal—"even from everlasting to everlasting, thou art God" (Psalm 90:2 b). (Also read Hebrews 1:8-12.) John 3:36 tells us, *"He that believeth on the Son HATH EVERLASTING LIFE:* and he that believeth not the Son shall not see life; but the wrath of God abideth on him."

To Know Christ Is to Follow Him

Jesus said, "When (the shepherd) putteth forth his own sheep, he goeth before them, and the sheep follow him: for they know his voice. And a stranger will they not follow, but will flee from him: for they know not the voice of strangers. . . . My sheep hear my voice, and I know them, and *they follow me"* (John 10:4, 5, 27).

What could be plainer? Regardless of what a man professes, if he has not heard, recognized and acknowledged the voice of God he is not saved and the Saviour does not know him as His own. No matter how many professions a man may make, if he does not follow Jesus he is not saved. He may follow, outwardly, for a little while, but in time he will show that he has not been made a new creature inwardly. He will be like those of whom Peter speaks in II Peter 2:22: "It is happened unto them according to the true proverb, The dog is turned to his own vomit again; and the sow that was washed to her wallowing in the mire."

Please notice this Scripture does not say that a *sheep* turned back into a dog or a sow. The dog was always a dog and the sow was always a sow. They were never regenerated and made sheep. If either the dog or the sow had been really *changed,* they would have had no desire to return to the "vomit" and the "mire"—in other words, the filth and degradation of the world. This Scripture is representative of people who only profess (but do not possess) eternal life—and there are literally millions of such professors. They are reformers, i. e., they reform and change their outward way of living, but they are not regenerated, born again children of God. But the true "sheep," the bona fide Christian, has a different story. He follows Christ, and "a stranger (he) will not follow."

The True Test of Christianity

Continuing to follow Christ is the true test

of a person's Christianity, the real proof that he has been born again and has not simply reformed and made a profession of Christianity. Is your greatest desire to follow Jesus, live a righteous life, and have a testimony that is above reproach? If not, then you need to be born again. Those who have been truly saved love to follow Jesus, and they will never *want* to turn back to sin.

If you will search the Scriptures, you will discover that nowhere from Genesis through Revelation does the Bible teach that it makes no difference how a Christian lives, or that one can live in sin and still get to heaven. Such teaching is foreign to true Bible doctrine. It does make a tremendous difference what the believer does, how he lives, and what sort of testimony he maintains before his fellowman. No matter how miserably a Christian fails in his attempt to live as becomes a child of God, his failure *never takes away his desire* to live right and to follow the will of God. His heart's desire is to bring glory to God and to live in a way that will honor Christ. The idea that he can live a careless life (live in sin) and still reach heaven never enters the heart and mind of the true Christian. Salvation plants within the heart of the believer a desire to live above sin. His ambition is to be "filled with the fruits of righteousness, which are by Jesus Christ, unto the glory and praise of God" (Phil. 1:11). Therefore, the true Christian is not concerned with how far he can stray into sin *and still get to heaven,* but rather with how much he can do for Christ and how he can establish a better Christian testimony in his daily living.

This does not mean that the believer is working *for* salvation, but *because* of it. Salvation is completely of grace, but to ignore the *responsibility* of a Christian *after* he is saved by grace is an unbalanced teaching, advanced by those who would put salvation back under law and place it on the basis of works. We who declare that salvation is by grace alone (apart from anything man can do) are accused of preaching a Gospel which makes for loose living and gives a license to sin; but the preaching of grace does no such thing! The Bible clearly declares: *"The grace of God that bringeth salvation hath appeared to all men, TEACHING US that, denying ungodliness and worldly lusts, we should live SOBERLY, RIGHTEOUSLY, AND GODLY, in this present world"* (Tit. 2:11, 12). Does that sound as if salvation by grace gives the believer a license to sin? In the words of the Apostle Paul, "Shall we continue in sin, that *grace* may abound? God forbid! *How shall we that are DEAD TO SIN, live any longer therein?"* (Rom. 6:1, 2). Those who say that "salvation by grace" gives a license to sin do not *know* the true grace of God at all!

Suppose we illustrate eternal life (salvation by grace, if you please) this way: Here I am, a poor lost sinner, born in sin and "shapen in iniquity" (Psalm 51:5). But God loved me enough to send His Son into the world to die for me, that I, through Him, might be saved from my sins. When I *accept* the salvation offered by grace, Jesus saves me, and I am now in His hands. In other words, my life is "hid with Christ in God" (Col. 3:3), which means that *God the Father* puts *His* hands around me too! Could there be more perfect security for the believer? Jesus Himself declared, "My Father . . . is greater than all; and *NO MAN is able to pluck them out of my Father's hand*" (John 10:29). *Even the devil* cannot touch me—unless he can loosen the hands of the Father and Son which hold and protect me. That is BIBLE FACT, not denominational doctrine. Paul testified, ". . . I KNOW whom I have believed, and am persuaded that *He is able to KEEP that which I have committed unto Him against that day*" (II Tim. 1:12).

Notice, however, *it is GOD who is faithful and able* to keep that which we have committed unto Him: *"GOD is faithful,* by whom ye were called unto the fellowship of His Son Jesus Christ our Lord" (I Cor. 1:9). I Corinthians 10:13 also declares, "There hath no temptation taken you but such as is common to man: but *God is faithful,* who will not suffer you to be tempted above that ye are able; but will with the temptation also make a way to escape, that ye may be able to bear it." You may well be afraid of church doctrine, but never be afraid of God's truth.

The "What If's . . . ."

Even well-meaning Christians are often so afraid of God's failing them that they put guards around the truth. They want to be prepared for the *"what if's"* in a Christian's life! *"What if* I sin?" they ask. Or *"What if* I fall into temptation?" Or *"What if* I fail in my efforts to understand and follow the will of God?" Without realizing it, they are trying to protect—not themselves, but GOD. They are actually saying, *"God can keep me saved IF* I continue to live a perfect life, if I never stumble or fail." God needs no protection. *He is greater than ALL.* He is greater than the Christian, greater than the devil, greater than all the emissaries of hell. I John 4:4 tells us, ". . . greater is He (the Holy Spirit) that is in you, than he (Satan and his emissaries) that is in the world."

We must remember, Christians, that we were "not redeemed with *corruptible* things, as silver and gold, from your vain conversation received by tradition from your fathers; *BUT WITH THE PRECIOUS BLOOD OF CHRIST,* as of a lamb without blemish and without spot: who verily was foreordained before the foundation of the world, but was manifest in these last times for you, who by Him do believe in God, that raised

Him up from the dead, and gave Him glory; that your faith and hope might be in God" (I Pet. 1:18-21).

Salvation from eternity to eternity does not depend upon us nor upon our works, but upon God and the finished work of Christ at Calvary. "Salvation belongeth unto the LORD . . ." (Psalm 3:8). ". . . Salvation is of the LORD" (Jonah 2:9). I repeat: SALVATION depends upon God, but our reward, our joy, and our blessings depend upon our faithfulness. (Read I Corinthians 3:11-15.)

Danger in Not Believing in God's Power to Save to the Uttermost

On one occasion I was trying to persuade a young lady to accept Christ. She frankly told me that she had no intention of being saved that night, because there was a party which she wanted to attend, and she knew that after attending that party she would have to be saved "over again." I asked her if she was trying to tell me that she had *been* saved, and she replied, *"Certainly. Many times!"* She told me that she would live for Christ for awhile, then when she wanted to slip back into the world, she did so. Very nonchalantly she said, "It's no problem. I do the things I want to do, knowing that I can get saved again afterward."

The Word of God teaches no such doctrine. On the contrary, the Word warns, "He, that being often reproved hardeneth his neck, *shall suddenly*

33

be destroyed, and that without remedy" (Prov. 29:1). The young lady I have just mentioned may have been taught wrong doctrine; but she really had no excuse for such careless living because she had the open Bible, and had she searched the Scriptures she would have seen that "there is a way that *seemeth right* unto a man, but *the end thereof are the ways of death*" (Prov. 16:25).

Because of the fact that church doctrine can be misused, misconstrued and wrongly applied, we must base our beliefs upon *"Thus saith the LORD."* When we base our beliefs upon God's Word we should stand fast and not misuse the truth upon which we have our faith. It is absolute fact that Scriptures relating to the subject of eternal life have been misused from one extreme to the other—i. e., by those who say that grace covers all and gives a license to sin, and also by those who maintain that each time they sin God casts them out. If both groups spent more time in thanking God for His glorious salvation and in trying to win lost souls, they would not have time to argue such doctrinal points!

A Solemn Warning to Christians

We have already established the fact that it is of utmost importance how a Christian lives. Every child of God who has grown cold and indifferent toward God needs to be awakened to the necessity of doing something about his spiritual life. God wants His children to live in such a way that they will not bring reproach to the name of Christ. Therefore the Word issues plain warnings to Christians—warnings against loss of influence, warnings against loss of reward, warnings to avoid chastening, and warnings against committing the sin unto death. Most assuredly we are warned against worldliness, against compromising with the world or becoming contaminated by it. We are also warned against becoming "lukewarm" Christians.

We are living in troublesome times. Many youths who are enthusiastic over "religion" are only "turning on" to something new; they are not truly accepting Christ as Saviour. Many older Christians have become tired and discouraged over the modernistic trend in our churches. Preachers—even fundamental preachers—are turning to "programs" and "things" to raise money to support their churches, giving suppers and parties, sponsoring ball games, and various other endeavors, instead of praying and trusting God to meet the needs of the church while the preacher gives his time and efforts to preaching the true Word in order to draw sinners to salvation through faith in the finished work of Christ.

This is a day when Christians need to remember that God is still on the throne, and we, as individuals, can and should stay true to the Word, true to God, and unspotted from the world. To do less is to invite chastisement, for there is a reckoning day coming when Christians who do not stand true to the unadulterated Gospel of the grace of God will wish they had! Ephesians 2:8, 9 tells us that we are saved *by grace, through faith,* "and that not of yourselves: *it is the GIFT of God:* not of works, lest any man should boast." But II Corinthians 5:10 warns that "we must all appear before the judgment seat of Christ; that every one may receive the things done in his body, *according to that he hath done, whether it be good or bad!"*

It is wonderful to be saved and have the assurance of eternal life; but with the wonderful miracle of the new birth there are also responsibilities—the responsibility to live above reproach and in so doing let our light so shine before men that they may see our good works and glorify our Father which is in heaven (Matt. 5:16). In this day, however, Christians are very lax in their daily life—and there is still *greater* laxity on the part of preachers in failing to preach against worldliness.

"Love Not the World"

The Scripture warns emphatically: *"LOVE NOT THE WORLD, neither the things that are in the world.* If any man love the world, the love of the Father is not in him. For all that is in the world, the lust of the flesh, and the lust of the eyes, and the pride of life, is not of the Father, but is of the world" (I John 2:15, 16).

Shall we look into these verses a bit more

closely? What is meant here by "love not *the world*"? It does not mean the world of *matter,* nor does it refer to the world of *nature*—even though, in spite of the curse, nature provides beauty that words cannot describe. We know that the "world" spoken of here is not the world of *people,* as such, because in John 3:16 we are told that God *so loved* the world that He gave His only begotten Son to die for the *sins* of the world—and certainly He does not want us to hate people. We are to hate sin and hate the ways of the sinner, but God loves all men and He commands US to love all men, especially they "of the household of faith."

What then IS "the world" we are to "love not"? The meaning here is simply that we are not to love anything IN this world that is alienated from God, whether it be "things," or people, or influences. *Satan* is "the *prince* of this world" (John 14:30), he is "the god of this world" (II Cor. 4:4), and "the whole world lieth in wickedness"— or, "lieth in the wicked one" (I John 5:19).

The systems of this world are in the hands of Satan—and sad but so, the vast majority of *people* are in his hands; but even though spiritually-minded people are in the minority, with JESUS we are always the *majority,* and we will win in the end because we are with Him who IS the victory!

The more lightly we cling to things of this

world, the tighter grip we have on God and things eternal. The Scripture here makes it crystal-clear that the world can draw the love of the believer away from the Father. When a Christian begins participating in worldly amusements, attending questionable places, and keeping company with unbelievers, he will soon discover that his love for God, his interest in God's Word and in fellowship with other believers, have begun to slip away. Prayer meeting, revival night, Sunday school and worship will become of secondary concern, and one sad day, all too late, that person will wake up to the fact that his joy and peace have gone. Exactly when it happened he may not know; it may have happened so gradually that he was not aware of it until it was too late.

The most miserable person on earth is the Christian who is out of fellowship with God and out of God's will, as Peter was the night he cursed, blasphemed, and denied his Lord. But when Jesus looked at him so tenderly, Peter went out and wept bitterly in repentance. In my experience in evangelistic meetings down through the years, the most bitter tears I have seen shed were not tears of sinners, but tears of *backsliders*. The Christian who has known God and served Him in full surrender, and then allowed the cares of the world to dampen his fervor and zeal for God and the things of God, is of all people most miserable.

When Paul was in prison he said, "Demas hath

forsaken me, having loved this present world"
(II Tim. 4:10). There is no neutral ground here;
the believer cannot love God completely and love
the world any at all. One bit of love for the
world, and the spiritual fulness of complete surrender begins to slowly ebb away.

The world and its attractions are all about us,
always bidding for the testimony of fine young
Christians. The devil takes great joy in causing a
strong Christian to become weak. There are some
believers whom Satan seldom bothers because they
do not cause him too much worry, they do not
threaten his program; but strong Christians are
always his targets and he puts countless snares
and pitfalls in their way. Therefore the admonition
to those who have "overcome the wicked one" is
to *"love not the world, neither the things that are
IN the world."*

I would emphasize again that this does not
refer to the *earth* as such. This globe which God
created has nothing to hurt souls. It is not a sin
to love nature (as long as we do not *worship*
nature). Surely the Lord Jesus loved the beauty
of the out-of-doors. In His Sermon on the Mount
He said, ". . . Consider the lilies of the field, how
they grow; they toil not, neither do they spin:
and yet I say unto you, That *even Solomon in all
his glory was not arrayed like one of these!"*
(Matt. 6:28, 29).

The *world systems* to which this Scripture in

I John 2:15 refers began back when "Cain went out from the presence of the Lord" (Gen. 4:16). He built a city, and from that day forward the systems of this world began to attract the souls of men, offering pleasures and many things that promised satisfaction without God. Satan has made it more attractive and more convenient to go to hell today than ever before! There are more species of attractions to lure people away from God and crowd God out of their lives. The devil and his cohorts take no time off; they work overtime, scheming, planning, "programming," devising new things to keep man away from God.

God's Word tells us that just before the flood "the wickedness of man was great in the earth, and . . . every imagination of the thoughts of his heart was only evil continually. And it repented the Lord that He had made man on the earth, and it grieved Him at His heart. And the Lord said, I will destroy man whom I have created from the face of the earth; both man, and beast, and the creeping thing, and the fowls of the air; for it repenteth me that I have made them" (Gen. 6:5-7).

Noah found grace in the eyes of the Lord, and he and his family were saved from the flood; but when they came out of the ark they brought with them *the same flesh* that had led man into such vileness as to make the flood necessary, and wickedness quickly started multiplying again.

Some people think of "the world" as the old-fashioned saloon, gambling halls, and the street of forgotten men and women; but Satan does not operate in these places alone. Many times he appears as "an angel of light" (II Cor. 11:14). He operates in the world of arts and culture, appealing to the flesh through these things; and even dedicated believers often find themselves attracted to and spending entirely too much time in things which the average Christian would call "harmless." It is not uncommon for the business world to become a stumbling block and a snare to the believer. We must be on guard at all times against the evils of this world. In John 17:15 Jesus said, "I pray not that thou shouldest take them out of the world, but that thou shouldest keep them from the evil."

Many good men have made mistakes which have been fruitful of much evil. Association with the ungodly always means danger, damage and distress to the man of God, whether he be preacher or layman. Worldly association invariably works mischief to the child of God. We cannot touch fire without being burned and blackened—and the greater tragedy lies in the fact that in defiling *ourselves* we also defile others! Make no mistake, no Christian is strong enough to escape the consequences of worldly association.

Worldliness robs a Christian of JOY. As a parasite sucks away the life of a plant by living upon its sap, causing the leaves to wither and die, so will association with the world cause the Christian to lose the joy of salvation. As the plant becomes lifeless and useless under the parasite's attack, so will the Christian who walks with the world lose his testimony and fulfill the devil's design instead of furthering the cause of Christ.

Worldliness will act as a CLOUD to hide the presence of the Lord. Some Christians wonder why they cannot pray effectively, or why they do not feel God's presence. Could it be that they have allowed the world to come between them and the face of Jesus? Remember that *Abraham* had no communication with God nor revelation from God as long as he dwelt in Egypt.

Worldliness is a DAMPER to quench our zeal for the Lord. If you are acquainted with the workings of a furnace, you know that to turn the damper down will cause the fire to die down and burn less brightly. Thus will association with the world dampen the zeal of the Christian and lessen his service to Christ. The spirit of the world and the Spirit of God do not work in harmony.

Worldliness disturbs the PEACE OF GOD within the Christian's heart. When we are saved we are *at peace WITH God,* and nothing can change that (Rom. 5:1); but by our daily living we can also have *the peace OF God* (Phil. 4:7). This is peace of the soul, a peace that comes through blessed fellowship with our Lord; but not all Christians enjoy the *peace OF God* because of failure to pray and to read the Word, and because of failure to live as Christians *should* live. If we want this peace of God, this quietness of soul, we must live in a way that is pleasing to Him, a life separated from the world.

Worldliness is as a TARNISH that dims the Word of God. Of course, in reality, nothing can tarnish the Word because it is pure, holy, and forever settled in heaven (Psalm 119:89). But for the careless Christian, appreciation of the Word of God will be dulled, its challenge will diminish, through association with the world. To neglect prayerfully studying the Word is a sure sign that the things of this world have interfered. The Word is precious. It is food to the soul, a light to our pathway; and it is by the Word that we grow in grace. We dare not allow worldliness to lessen our interest in it.

Worldliness HINDERS the flow of the power of God. Participation in things of the world will hinder the inflow and the outflow of spiritual power in the life of the Christian. This is probably the answer, many times, to the question, "What's wrong with me?" Spiritual power cannot flow through channels that are clogged with the debris of worldliness.

Worldliness mars Christian TESTIMONY. When a Christian walks in the counsel of the ungodly, the company of the ungodly will be a retarding influence on the believer's fellowship with the

Lord, just as Solomon's "strange" wives changed his heart from following the Lord (I Kings 11:1-3). A believer who becomes involved in worldly activities and associations is of little or no use to God and he misses the joy of sweet fellowship that comes to those who are faithful stewards.

When we live in the presence of the Lord He stands *between* us and the world and we are kept from its contaminating influence. It is a false premise to suppose that a person can be a consecrated child of God and yet mix with the world. The New Testament teaches that believers recognize that Christ died to *deliver* us from the world (Gal. 1:4); that we are *saved* from the world (Gal. 6:14); that we are no longer *OF* the world (John 17:16); and that we obey God by *not loving* the world (I John 2:15-17).

Works

The more a Christian realizes and recognizes his *position IN CHRIST* the greater will be his desire to work for Christ. "A good tree cannot bring forth evil fruit, neither can a corrupt tree bring forth good fruit" (Matt. 7:18).

James 2:17-20 makes it clear that those who have faith in Christ will produce good works: "Even so faith, if it hath not works, is dead, being alone. Yea, a man may say, Thou hast faith, and I have works: shew me thy faith without thy works, and I will shew thee my faith by my works. Thou believest that there is one God; thou doest well: the devils also believe, and tremble. But wilt thou know, O vain man, that *faith without works is dead?"*

But what about James 2:21 which reads: "Was not Abraham . . . justified by works, when he offered Isaac his son upon the altar?" Does this not teach that we must work *to KEEP* our salvation? No, it does not. The Bible never contradicts itself, and Romans chapter 4 definitely—and plainly—teaches that we are *saved by FAITH*, not works.

In Romans 4:1-4 we read: "What shall we say then that Abraham our father, as pertaining to the flesh, hath found? For if Abraham were justified by works, he hath whereof to glory; but not before God. For what saith the Scripture? *Abraham believed God,* and it was counted unto him for righteousness. Now to him that worketh is the reward not reckoned of grace, but of debt."

The question here is simply this: "What then shall we say was gained by Abraham, our father after the flesh? What did he really gain and how did he gain it? If he was justified by works, then he has reason for boasting." But Paul hurries on to say, through the leading of the Holy Spirit, *"but NOT BEFORE GOD."* "Before God" is the key that unlocks the seeming conflict between the teaching of Paul and the teaching of James. *James* is speaking of justification *in the sight of men,* while *Paul* is speaking of justification *before*

Almighty God. That no flesh is justified by works *in the sight of God* is Paul's Gospel truth, while James points out that the man of faith *shows* his faith by his *works.* Faith, which only God can see, justifies the unbeliever in God's sight; but works testify to the eyes of men that we are believers and have exercised faith in God. We prove our faith by our works. James says, "Faith without works is dead," and I agree. I think you will, too, if you will weigh the matter. A person who is born again may not do much, he may not make a big show; but if he is truly saved he is alive unto God, and certainly there will be some movement or activity on his part to *prove* that he is alive unto God. The person who testifies that he has faith in God, and yet never does anything to prove that faith, has certainly put a big question mark around his profession in the eyes of his fellowmen.

Only God can see the heart, and certainly God knows who has saving faith and who does not exercise saving faith. But *we* know people only by their fruits and their works. So there is no conflict between the teaching of Paul and the teaching of James. Paul is speaking concerning faith before God. James is speaking concerning faith that produces works that can be seen of men. The Scriptures prove that a saved person has a new heart, new desires, new ambitions. He will produce good works, and he will have no desire to turn back into the world.

Difficult Passages of Scripture

There are verses of Scripture which disturb many people, people who sincerely want the assurance of salvation. It is true that the Bible contains many warnings addressed to Christians, but some teachers *apply* to Christians many other Scriptures which, in the true interpretation, do not apply to Christians at all. For instance, certain Scriptures are used by the advocates of the doctrine that a person is lost every time he sins and must be saved all over again. But the Scriptures so used are taken out of context and wrongly applied, whereas if the passage is read in its entirety and under the teaching of the Holy Spirit, it would present absolutely no ground for confusion.

By like token, many of the Scriptures used to prove "once saved, always saved" actually have nothing to do with the doctrine of eternal life. We are instructed in the Word, "Study to shew thyself approved unto God, a workman that needeth not to be ashamed, *RIGHTLY DIVIDING the Word of Truth*" (II Tim. 2:15). We are also instructed that "no prophecy of the Scripture is of any *private* interpretation" (II Pet. 1:20).

Since Scripture can be twisted to make it fit "pet doctrines," as we examine some of these Scriptures we will lay aside all church doctrine and listen only to what the Word says. In giving a few Scriptures which are often misinterpreted,

I will refer, in my explanations, to Evangelist Oliver B. Greene's Commentaries; and I ask you to bear in mind that the comments on these passages are strictly in an effort to *explain* them, not to uphold a doctrine or render a "private interpretation."

John 8:31:—

In John 8:31 we read: "Then said Jesus to those Jews which believed on Him, If ye continue in my Word, then are ye my disciples indeed." This verse often raises the question, "Is not this a condition for permanent discipleship?" Certainly. But it only shows who are the saved and who are the unsaved. The man who is truly saved will continue to follow Jesus—but he does not have to continue in discipleship in order to *keep* saved. He continues to follow Jesus because he *is* saved.

You will notice, in verse 30 of this chapter from John's Gospel, as Jesus *"spake THESE WORDS,* many believed on Him." "These words" indicate the entire discourse of Jesus at this time, beginning with verse 12 of this chapter. No doubt there was much in His teaching that reminded the people of prophecies from the Old Testament, and thus "many *believed on Him"*—but only with intellectual belief. Their hearts were unchanged, they did not believe on Him as Saviour and Lord. This is proved by their later actions, up to the time of His crucifixion. It is not *believing ABOUT*

48

Jesus that makes men sons of God; it is truly *believing ON Him,* trusting from the heart: "For with the heart man believeth unto righteousness; and with the mouth confession is made unto salvation" (Rom. 10:10).

Passing impulses and emotion do not make true Christians. Discipleship depends upon permanent application of the Word. *"If ye continue in my Word"* does not mean that these people had *accepted* the Word—at least not in the terms of "except ye eat my flesh and drink my blood," the actual appropriation of the Word. What Jesus was saying here is simply this: "If you receive me in truth you will take a firm stand and *continue* in the Word which you have received." The same truth is expressed in many other places in the New Testament—as in Romans 8:1 where Paul says, "There is therefore now no condemnation to them which are in Christ Jesus, *who walk not after the flesh, but after the Spirit."* You will notice Paul did not say, *"IF* they walk not after the flesh," but *"WHO WALK NOT after the flesh."* Since Christ is in the believer, the believer walks in the Spirit. We are children of light and we walk in the light because Christ abides within. The proof of true faith, according to our present verse, is walking in faith, abiding in the Word.

John 6:66:—

What about John 6:66, where we read that many

49

of Christ's disciples "went back, and walked no more with Him"? This has nothing to do with our subject of Eternal Life, and certainly it does not prove that a born again person will turn back and walk with Jesus no more. This "turning back" of disciples has occurred all down through the centuries, in all forms of religion, both true and false. The Greek word translated "disciple" means *a learner*, or *pupil*. I think Jesus Himself made clear the difference between one who is only a disciple, a learner, and one who is a true believer. When many who had followed Jesus turned their backs on Him and "walked no more with Him," they expressed disappointment in their expectations of Him. No doubt they had thought that He would soon be crowned King and would deliver them from the tyranny of Rome; but at the close of His discourse on the bread of life they gave up all hope of seeing their ambitions fulfilled in Him, and they rejected Him. These people were never born again. They were simply following Jesus for what they could get out of it, hoping that eventually He would become King and they would profit by having been associated with Him.

Ezekiel 18:24:—

Ezekiel 18:24 elicits questions from many people. In that verse we read, "When the righteous turneth away from his righteousness, and committeth iniquity, and doeth according to all the abominations

50

that the wicked man doeth, shall he live? All his righteousness that he hath done shall not be mentioned: in his trespass that he hath trespassed, and in his sin that he hath sinned, in them shall he die." I would assure you that in this Dispensation of Grace this verse from Ezekiel's prophecy has nothing to do with the soul's salvation. Do not separate this verse from its context. Go back and read the *entire eighteenth chapter* of Ezekiel. In verse 21 you will note these words: "If the wicked will turn from all his sins that he hath committed, and *keep all my statutes,* and do that which is *lawful and right,* he shall surely live, he shall not die."

Is that GRACE? Indeed not. *It is LAW.* It is strange that any enlightened person would use Ezekiel 18:24 to prove—or *disprove*—the fact of a soul's eternal salvation in this glorious Dispensation of Grace!

Hebrews 6:4-6:—

Possibly the most crucial—and most misunderstood—verses in all of God's Word are Hebrews 6:4-6, quoted here for our study:

"It is impossible for those who were once enlightened, and have tasted of the heavenly gift, and were made partakers of the Holy Ghost, and have tasted the good Word of God, and the powers of the world to come, if they shall fall away, to renew them again unto repentance; seeing they crucify to themselves the Son of God afresh, and put Him to an open shame."

These verses are among the most solemn in all the Word of God. They furnish a fierce battle-ground among students of theology. The hottest fight extant between religious groups rages around these verses. It is a known and established fact that a vast number of religious people believe it is possible for a blood-washed, truly born again believer to sin and backslide to the extent of being lost, beyond forgiveness, and eternally damned. Most of these dear people have their minds made up; it is futile to argue with them—and they use these verses as proof of their doctrine.

I refuse to argue the Scriptures. I use *Bible* terms, not the language of denominations. We are commanded to prove all things (I Thess. 5:21); we are clearly instructed to *study*, rightly dividing the Word of Truth (II Tim. 2:15). I readily confess that it is not always easy to discover the perfect consistency of one Scripture with another; yet we who believe the Word of God must hold fast to the unerring harmony and integrity of His infallible, indestructible, forever-settled truth. We must keep in mind that we are finite and will never fully understand all the Word of God until we sit at the feet of Jesus to be taught of Him in that grand and glorious heavenly Bible class.

We must make sure of whom the Holy Spirit is speaking in our passage from Hebrews 6. Is He speaking of born again souls? or of unregenerate souls? What is meant by the statement *"if they shall fall away"*? What is meant by the assertion that *"it is impossible to renew them again to repentance"*?

Not one of the five expressions used in Hebrews 6:4-6 is equivalent to partaking of Divine life; nor are all of them together the equivalent of partaking, as Peter says, "of divine nature." A sinner may be moved in any one or in ALL of the five ways pointed out here, and yet remain an unbeliever. In the physical world, where there is *life* there is *growth.* The growth may be slow, but life *does* produce, and when it ceases to produce it is deteriorating—and that is *death.* If there is no growth, there is no life. The same is true in the spiritual realm. Jesus said that some bring forth thirty, some sixty, some a hundredfold—but He did not say "Some bring forth *NO fruit* at all."

We need to pay close attention to the opening words of verse 4: *"For it is impossible . . . ."* These words take us back to what has been discussed in the previous verses, where we learned that there were some who professed to be Christians although they still clung to the Levitical system of ordinances and typology. These were professed believers who still held on to the old economy of the law, still trusting in the Old Testament sacrifices and Mosaic institutions, which were only shadows and types. They saw Jesus as the great Teacher and the great Healer—but they would not accept His death, burial, and resurrection "according to the Scriptures."

Paul is speaking here of persons who were warned in verses 1 and 2 of Hebrews 6, persons who became *learners*, yet returned again and again to the rituals of Judaism. They may even have professed to be Christians, but they were still Judaizers, returning to ceremonial washings, laying on of hands, laying again the foundation of "repentance from dead works." We read the positive declaration in Romans 10:4 that *"Christ is the END of the law for righteousness to every one that believeth."* These people never actually and experimentally put their faith in the finished work of the Lord Jesus Christ as the Son of God and Saviour of sinners. They never fully realized and accepted the truth of Colossians 2:10—"ye are complete in HIM."

". . . those who were once enlightened . . . ." This describes the general effect of the Gospel upon the mind of the hearer: "But call to remembrance the former days, in which, after ye were illuminated, ye endured a great fight of afflictions" (Heb. 10:32). The reference to those who were once enlightened has to do with the illumination given when the Gospel is first heard with the ear and received with the mind—we might call it "head belief."

All who have ever made a profession, genuine

or counterfeit, were once *enlightened*—otherwise they would have never united with a local church and professed to receive Jesus as Saviour. There are many members of the average church who have been "enlightened," they have united with the church, they have followed Christ in baptism, and many of them give liberally of their money—yet inwardly they do not possess life that produces "fruits meet for repentance"—fruits automatically produced by one who has truly repented of sin and been born again. Any person who has heard the Gospel of the grace of God has been "enlightened," for the Word of God is a lamp, a light, "the power of God unto salvation to every one that believeth" (Rom. 1:16).

Those to whom Paul directs the solemn warning recorded here are said to have *tasted* of the heavenly gift—and what IS "the heavenly gift"? In II Corinthians 9:15 Paul speaks of God's "unspeakable gift." In John 3:16 we read of God's Gift to a lost world, and in Ephesians 2:8 we read that we are saved by grace through faith, *"the gift of God."* The "heavenly gift," then, unquestionably refers to salvation in Christ. Does this mean that these people were truly born again? The Christian certainly has "tasted"—but he has done *more* than taste. To *taste* is to have a *personal experience* of, in contrast with mere *report;* but tasting does not include *eating,* much less digesting and turning into nourishment what is so tasted.

Eternal life becomes ours—not by "tasting," but by *eating*, by assimilating. One may taste—and not EAT. One may taste—and not assimilate that which he tastes. But when we think of *eating* we think of tasting, chewing, and swallowing the substance tasted. Thus, when we receive "the engrafted Word" (James 1:21) we actually *assimilate* the Word, which is spirit and life (John 6:63). "Tasting" is not enough; we must EAT. And these people of whom Paul writes are said to have "tasted."

In Revelation 10:9, 10 John the Beloved said, "I went unto the angel, and said unto him, Give me the little book. And he said unto me, Take it, and eat it up; and it shall make thy belly bitter, but it shall be in thy mouth sweet as honey. And I took the little book out of the angel's hand, and ate it up; and it was in my mouth sweet as honey: and as soon as I had eaten it, my belly was bitter."

These Hebrews had tasted of "the principles of the doctrine of Christ"—that is, "the word of the beginning of Christ"; but they were still practicing the precepts of Judaism, observing the typology of the Old Testament system. They had not received the gift of God—salvation by grace through faith in the finished work of Jesus. They had tasted but they had not eaten. They had heard about Jesus, they were mixing and mingling with the apostles and other Hebrews who were genuinely born again, and in so doing they certainly had had a taste of Christ and His saving power and grace.

"*. . . and were made partakers of the Holy Ghost.*" This statement certainly sounds as though it would be made concerning a born again Christian; but again, the Greek verb *metechoo* from which the noun *metochous* is derived, means "to go along with." These people who had been "partakers" of the Holy Ghost had shared in the benefit of His supernatural operations and manifestations. They had not only witnessed the effects of the Holy Ghost in others, but by associating with these born again believers they had benefitted and enjoyed the blessings.

We know there can be no conviction APART FROM the Holy Spirit, and no man can become a Christian except the Holy Ghost draw him (John 6:44; 16:7-9). Therefore, when one hears the Gospel, recognizes his need of a Saviour—perhaps even to the point of uniting with some local church and submitting to the ritual of baptism—it can certainly be said that he "goes along" with the Holy Ghost; but it also could be that he does all of these things without becoming a partaker of divine nature.

These people of whom Paul was writing went along with Christianity *to a point*—and then turned back to Judaism. They were attempting to mix law and grace, which is impossible. Salvation is either all of grace, or no grace at all, according to Paul's teaching to the church at Galatia. It is by grace through faith *plus nothing* that we become the children of God.

"*...and have tasted the good Word of God...*" To taste the good Word of God as applied to these Hebrews seems to mean that they merely enjoyed the advantages of the new dispensation. Let me again emphasize that to taste is not to *assimilate;* and the mystery revealed to the Apostle Paul, hidden through the ages of eternity, is "Christ in you, the hope of glory" (Col. 1:26, 27). It is possible to "taste, and see that the Lord is good," without assimilating, eating, or receiving Christ by faith, without allowing Him to come into the heart. Any person who has been convicted religiously to the point of uniting with a church or embracing some phase of religion has done so because he heard (tasted, was enlightened to) the goodness of the Word of God.

Many *unbelievers* have tasted of the good Word of God to the point where they say grace at meals, they say (or read) prayers before going to bed—and *"the good Word of God"* here probably refers to God's promises which are always consoling and inspiring of confidence (Heb. 10:35; Zech. 1:13).

As true as it is that the five experiences mentioned in verses 4 and 5 are experiences that Christians do encounter, they may also be had by those who only *profess* to be saved. But observe that these activities fall far short of true Christian experiences. For instance, nothing is said of their having been "quickened with Christ" to new life in Him, or that they were indwelt by the Holy Spirit or sealed by Him unto the day of redemption. It is not said that they *believed* in the Lord Jesus Christ, the eternal Word of God, and they are not given the characteristics mentioned in Scripture concerning the truly born again. Rather, all things mentioned as pertaining to them could be applied to anyone who had *professed* Christianity but fallen short of grace and returned to Judaism.

Paul goes further to say that these have *"tasted . . . the powers of the world to come."* They tasted—but they did not fully receive, they did not fully embrace.

Ephesians 1:13 describes the Holy Spirit's relationship to the believer: "In whom (Christ) ye also trusted, after that ye heard the Word of Truth, the Gospel of your salvation: in whom also after that ye believed, ye were sealed with that Holy Spirit of promise."

In our present passage there is not one word about the new birth. Do you really believe that God in His love, Jesus in His saving grace, would put a passage in the New Testament to confuse people and frighten those who have truly been born again? Indeed He would not! If those described in verses 4, 5, and 6 are truly born again believers, how simple it would have been for the

Holy Spirit to have said, "For it is impossible for those *who were once born again,* if they fall away, to renew them again unto repentance."

But this is not what the Word declares. These were not genuine believers, they were never born again. Here is described a peculiar, singular—though by no means uncommon—group who *professed much* but *possessed nothing.* They went to the very door of salvation but refused to enter; therefore, *they fell away.*

In the statement *"if they shall fall away"* the Greek language is much stronger than in Matthew 7:27 where Jesus spoke of the house built on the sand, "and great was the fall of it." By "falling away" we are to plainly understand that this is not speaking of an occasional falling into sin, nor of the renunciation of some of the Christian principles, but it is an *utter and complete* falling away, utter abandonment of the faith. It is willful turning from God, turning one's back on God's revealed truth, truth made known through the light of the Word. It has to do with utter repudiation of the truth, referred to in I Timothy 1:19 as making "shipwreck" of the faith.

These persons, having been exposed to the light, the truth, and the power of the Gospel, openly and knowingly declare total renunciation of the truth and the principles of Christianity. It is impossible to renew such ones unto repentance.

A born again person not only repents of sin,

but is "created IN Christ Jesus" (Eph. 2:10), becoming "a new creature" (II Cor. 5:17). Repentance signifies a change of mind (Matt. 21:29; Rom. 11:29). *Judas* repented—but his repentance did not produce the things which accompany salvation (Matt. 27:3-5). His was "sorrow of the world," and "the sorrow of the world worketh death" (II Cor. 7:10). These persons had not been created new in Christ Jesus through the miracle of the new birth and the power of the Holy Ghost. They had not believed "the truth as it is in Jesus."

It is very clear that *"impossible"* is the true meaning here. Some things are definitely impossible with God because of His nature. There are some things God cannot do—e. g., God cannot *lie* (Heb. 6:18; Tit. 1:2). He cannot *pardon sin* (Nah. 1:3) without an innocent substitute that brings satisfaction to His holiness and justice. (Also study I Samuel 15:28, 29.)

Saving faith is impossible apart from hearing the Word. Study Romans 10:13-17, where it is clearly pointed out that one *MUST hear* the Gospel before he can *believe* the Gospel and exercise saving faith. It is impossible for God to grant salvation to any person before that person hears, believes, and receives the Word.

Likewise, *salvation apart from repentance* is a divine impossibility (Luke 13:3, 5). It is necessary to repent—or perish. God cannot accept one into His family apart from repentance. That is the "impossibility" primarily intended here.

It is impossible to "renew unto repentance" one who has heard and rejected the Gospel of the grace of God, for there IS no other Gospel, there is no further message of repentance. *Christ is the END of the law for righteousness to all who believe.* He is made unto us wisdom, righteousness, sanctification, and redemption. In Him is our sufficiency, in Him we are complete. Christ—crucified, buried, risen again—had been preached to these Hebrews, but they denounced Him as an impostor, and there was no other name through and by which they COULD be saved. They publicly renounced the Christ of Calvary, thus rendering themselves hopeless; and the only thing that can be said about such persons is, "Ephraim is joined to idols: *let him alone*" (Hos. 4:17).

Hebrews 10:26-29: —

Another often misunderstood passage is Hebrews 10:26-29: "For if we sin wilfully after that we have received the knowledge of the truth, there remaineth no more sacrifice for sins, but a certain fearful looking for of judgment and fiery indignation, which shall devour the adversaries. He that despised Moses' law died without mercy under two or three witnesses: of how much sorer punishment, suppose ye, shall he be thought worthy, who hath trodden under foot the Son of God, and hath counted the blood of the covenant, wherewith

He was sanctified, an unholy thing, and hath done despite unto the Spirit of grace?"

"If we sin wilfully . . . ." Here again the Holy Spirit warns those who have received the knowledge of the truth, those who have been "enlightened." The sin referred to here is the sin of willful apostasy—the willful abandoning of a professed faith. Those who had professed to embrace Christianity, turning their backs on Judaism, had automatically turned their backs on the legal sacrifices for sin; and now if they abandoned Christianity to return to Judaism they HAD no sacrifice at all! There IS no other sacrifice save the *one sacrifice* Christ made, and those guilty of turning their backs on His sacrifice could not find a second sacrifice. Such a person could expect nothing but the wrath of God and divine judgment.

The Greek verb here translated "sin" is in the present, continuous tense, indicating not a series of acts or the practicing of different acts of sin, but a *condition*.

The Greek word translated "wilfully" is a very strong word meaning *deliberately*. In other words, the person has thought it through, weighed it, and settled his mind. The language here does not signify a sudden impulse, but settled intention after thorough thought. This word is used only twice in the entire New Testament—here, and in I Peter 5:2, where it is translated "willingly." Willful sinning is the sin of apostasy.

There are those who argue that this refers to a person who has been genuinely born again; but receiving the *knowledge* of the truth is quite different from receiving *the finished work of Christ by faith* and thus being born of His Spirit. To receive the knowledge of the truth is simply to have a mental apprehension of the doctrines of the Christian faith—not necessarily to *practice* these doctrines, but to know them from the mental standpoint.

The Hebrews who professed to embrace Christianity openly renounced the Levitical sacrifices that had been offered under the Mosaic economy. NOW if they turned from their professed faith they automatically renounced the sacrifice of the blood of Jesus; and since He died and now lives to die no more, they could never claim HIS sacrifice again, because He can never again be sacrificed! Therefore "THERE REMAINETH NO MORE SACRIFICE FOR SINS!"

"...he...who...hath counted the blood of the covenant, wherewith He (Jesus) was sanctified, an unholy thing...." You will note that I have capitalized the pronoun "He," for it is my opinion that this is the correct interpretation of the Scripture and not, as some say, that the second "he" in this verse is speaking of a person who at one time was a child of God. Jesus Christ *Himself* was sanctified and set apart unto God, to be an eternal High Priest *through the blood of the covenant offered unto God.* It was of this sanctification that Jesus speaks in John 17:19:

"For their sakes (for the sake of those whom the Father had given Him in the world) *I sanctify myself,* that they also might be sanctified through the truth.'' Jesus sanctified Himself that WE might be sanctified; and the person who hears the glorious Gospel of the death, burial, and resurrection of Christ and still turns his back on Him, by so doing declares the blood to be common, unholy—and such a sin will damn the soul of any person guilty of it!

The Gospel message that enlightens men unto salvation is the message of Calvary:

Calvary cost God His beloved Son.

Calvary cost Jesus His life's blood—the Just shedding His blood for the unjust, that we might be born again.

Calvary is the theme of the Word of God.

Calvary was God's best, on display for man's worst.

Calvary was the most amazing and most glorious act of all history—secular or sacred.

Yet Calvary is counted by some as an ordinary event and Jesus as just another martyr. Many mock and make fun of what they refer to as a "bloody, butcherhouse religion.'' It is no wonder the Holy Spirit declares that such sacrilege demands the sorest fiery judgment poured out by a holy God!

But there is more: A person having been exposed to the Gospel of the grace of God and then refusing to believe on the Lord Jesus Christ is said to have *"done despite unto the Spirit of grace."* To treat the Holy Spirit in such a shameful way involves sinning against the Father, the Son, *and* the Holy Spirit, because they are ONE in grace. God the Father loved us, God the Son died for us, God the Holy Spirit calls us and draws us to God.

The Holy Spirit came on the Day of Pentecost and He has been here ever since. He came to magnify Jesus—not to speak of Himself. (Study the sixteenth chapter of John.) When men come under the hearing of the Gospel, when the Spirit convicts them of their need of a Saviour and enlightens them that Christ died for the ungodly, and in spite of the Spirit's wooing they ignore His pleading and turn their backs upon the Word of God, they commit the sin of the apostate. Having received the knowledge of the truth, having trodden under foot the Son of God and counted the blood of the covenant common and unholy, having done despite to the Spirit of grace, nothing but judgment and eternal damnation could await such a person. There remains no other sacrifice.

Hebrews 3:14, 15:—

What about Hebrews 3:14 and 15 where we read: "For we are made partakers of Christ, if we hold the beginning of our confidence stedfast unto the end; while it is said, To day if ye will hear His voice, harden not your hearts, as in the provocation."

"... IF we hold the beginning of our confidence stedfast unto the end." Does our keeping saved depend upon the *"if"* in that statement? Here is the same truth declared in verse 6 of Hebrews chapter 3. By "holding fast the confidence and the rejoicing of the hope firm unto the end," we prove to ourselves and to the world that we are members of the body of Christ. Our salvation does not depend upon our holding fast, but we are steadfast BECAUSE we are saved. The same truth is found in Romans 8:1: "There is therefore now no condemnation to them which are in Christ Jesus, who walk not after the flesh, but after the Spirit." You will notice this does not say *"IF they walk not . . . ."* It is a definite statement: *"WHO walk NOT."* The walk is not a condition. They walk not after the flesh *because* they are not condemned, they are "in Christ Jesus."

"We are made partakers of Christ" — we are not *going to be* made partakers in the future; we ARE MADE partakers NOW, and we *prove* that we are partakers of Christ *"if we hold the beginning of our confidence stedfast unto the end."*

The Bible clearly teaches that those who are in Christ Jesus "walk not after the flesh, but after the Spirit" (Rom. 8:1). We walk after the Spirit and not after the flesh because we are in Christ Jesus. We do not live right in order to *become* Christians and reach heaven—we live right because we are saved and *on our way* to heaven. Our citizenship is in heaven and we are traveling toward our home. We are pilgrims and strangers on earth. We live right and walk right because we are *MADE right in our hearts.*

The greatest miracle known since the virgin birth of Jesus is the new birth of the individual who exercises faith in the finished work of the Son of God. The new birth is God's miracle. We are born of God (John 1:13), not by works of righteousness which we do, not through good living or good works. It is by God's power that we are born into His family.

When we are born again we become sons of God instantaneously.

"Beloved, NOW are we the sons of God" (I John 3:2).

"There is therefore NOW no condemnation to them which are in Christ Jesus..." (Rom. 8:1).

We "ARE dead," and our lives ARE hid "with Christ in God" (Col. 3:3).

We NOW "sit together in heavenly places in Christ Jesus" (Eph. 2:6, 7).

We ARE possessors of the Holy Spirit, led by the Spirit, assured by the Spirit (Rom. 8:9, 14, 16).

We ARE sealed by the Spirit "unto the day of redemption" (Eph. 4:30).

We ARE new creations in Christ Jesus (II Cor. 5:17).

We are NOW partakers of divine nature (II Pet. 1:4).

We HAVE an inheritance that is incorruptible, undefiled, and that cannot fade away, reserved for us in heaven (I Pet. 1:3-5).

I Corinthians 15:2: —

We find another "if" in I Corinthians 15:2, where Paul speaks of the Gospel "by which also ye are saved, *IF ye keep in memory what I preached unto you, unless ye have believed in vain."* This does not imply that salvation depends upon the individual's holding fast to the Gospel. If that were true, then we would not be saved by the free gift of God, the unmerited favor of His grace. Salvation is OF the Lord, BY the Lord, THROUGH the Lord, IN the Lord. Salvation is altogether THE LORD.

What the Holy Spirit is saying through Paul is simply this: If the Corinthians denied the truth of the bodily resurrection of Jesus Christ, that would be proof that they were NOT holding fast what Paul had taught them.

"...unless ye have believed in vain." The Greek word here translated "in vain" is *eike* and means "without cause, or to no purpose." That would be true if Christ had not been raised.

The whole thing in a nutshell is this: If Christ

did not rise from the dead then the message Paul preached had no grounds for truth—it was not valid, it was a lie; and they therefore had no reason to believe his message . . . *IF Christ had not been raised bodily from the grave.* The question here is not whether they would "hold on" or "hold to"—but if they did not believe in the bodily resurrection, then they had never believed from the heart.

Colossians 1:21-23:—

We find another "if" in Colossians 1:21-23: "And you, that were sometime alienated and enemies in your mind by wicked works, yet now hath He reconciled in the body of His flesh through death, to present you holy and unblameable and unreproveable in His sight: *IF YE CONTINUE in the faith* grounded and settled, and be not moved away from the hope of the Gospel, which ye have heard, and which was preached to every creature which is under heaven; whereof I Paul am made a minister."

The statement "if ye continue in the faith" does not suggest doubt, or that the Colossians may fall away from the faith. That is not the meaning at all. Paul is not teaching the Colossians that salvation depends upon *continuance in faith.* The truly born again, blood-washed believer *will continue* in faith.

In verse 23 Paul is admonishing the Colossian

believers to be grounded and settled in the faith—
the faith to which Jude refers, "which was once
delivered unto the saints" (Jude 3). (Read Ephesians 3:17; I Peter 5:10; and I Corinthians 15:58.)
Born again, blood-washed, saved-by-grace sons of
God are founded and fixed, and "shall not be
moved."

Many believers need to study and accept Ephesians 1:18: "The eyes of your understanding being
enlightened; that ye may know WHAT IS THE
HOPE OF HIS CALLING, and what the riches
of the glory of His inheritance in the saints."

A life of true faith in the finished work of Jesus
Christ, instead of faith in one's own ability or in
some religion, is a life of hope—and leads to glory.
True faith in the finished work of Jesus has a
conservative power. Such faith keeps the justified,
secures the one who is "hid with Christ in God"
(Col. 3:3) and who is continuously cleansed by the
precious blood of the Lamb (I John 1:7). The true
Bible fact that the believer is kept by the power
of God—yea, kept by God Himself—does not cause
the believer to live a careless life, but rather makes
him distrustful of himself and totally dependent
upon God. The believer knows the truth of the
warning, "Let him that thinketh he standeth take
heed lest he fall" (I Cor. 10:12).

The true believer also knows "There hath no
temptation taken you but such as is common to
man: but God is faithful, who will not suffer you

to be tempted above that ye are able; but will with the temptation also make a way to escape, that ye may be able to bear it" (I Cor. 10:13).

In verse 23 Paul admonishes the Colossians, ". . . and be not moved away from the hope of the Gospel." Just what is the Gospel? If we are admonished not to be moved away from the *hope* of the Gospel, what IS the Gospel in the first place? The best place to find the answer is in God's Word. In I Corinthians 15:1-8 Paul says:

"Moreover, brethren, I declare unto you THE GOSPEL which I preached unto you, which also ye have received, and wherein ye stand; by which also ye are *saved,* if ye keep in memory what I preached unto you, unless ye have believed in vain. For I delivered unto you first of all that which I also received, how that *CHRIST DIED FOR OUR SINS according to the Scriptures; and that HE WAS BURIED, and that HE ROSE AGAIN THE THIRD DAY according to the Scriptures:* and that He was seen of Cephas, then of the twelve: after that, He was seen of above five hundred brethren at once; of whom the greater part remain unto this present, but some are fallen asleep. After that, He was seen of James; then of all the apostles. *And last of all HE WAS SEEN OF ME ALSO, as of one born out of due time."*

Paul preached *the Gospel.* The Corinthians were *saved* by the Gospel, they were *standing* in the Gospel; but what did he preach? He preached what he received: *How that Christ died for our sins according to the Scriptures.* He was buried *according to the Scriptures;* He rose again and was seen by many men, *as recorded in the Scriptures.* Paul preached a crucified, buried, risen, ascended, living Lord. *That is the Gospel*—but it must be *"according to the Scriptures."*

The errorists in the Colossian community were teaching that Jesus was not the God-Man, that He did not actually die, that He was not actually raised, that He was some sort of spirit-being. Such teaching is not the Gospel. It is error, and it will damn all who believe it. Thus Paul admonished the Colossians to continue in the Gospel, to hold fast their faith in the death, burial, and resurrection of Christ—faith in the one Mediator, the Man Christ Jesus.

Paul goes further: He said, ". . . which ye have heard . . . ." That is, "You are informed concerning the Gospel. I have preached the Gospel to you, Timothy has preached the Gospel to you, Epaphras has preached the Gospel to you. You are not in the dark, you are children of light; so walk in the light. *Continue* in the light, and pay no attention to these errorists."

The statement, "which was preached to every creature which is under heaven" may confuse some, but it simply means to every creature (to the whole world) known in that day. That did not take in the earth's surface as we know it today, nor the multiplied millions we have on earth today. Paul is simply saying that the Gospel had been preached throughout that area to all the people and there was no excuse for ignorance concerning it. He closes the statement by saying, "... whereof I Paul am made a minister." He was not a denomination-called preacher. He was not a self-made preacher, nor a seminary-manufactured preacher. He was a *God-called* preacher, ordained of God, sent by God—and he preached the Gospel of God without fear, favor, or apology. He pleaded with the Colossians to stand by the Gospel "which ye have heard."

II Thessalonians 2:3:—

What about II Thessalonians 2:3? "Let no man deceive you by any means: for that day shall not come, except there come a falling away first, and that man of sin be revealed, the son of perdition." Paul declares, "... except there come a falling away." The words here should read "except THE APOSTASY come." *"The"* is a definite article, pointing to a specific apostasy that MUST come preceding the unveiling of the Man of Sin. And when THE apostasy comes and the Man of Sin is revealed, then the peoples on earth may rest assured that they are in the Great Tribulation and that the Day of the Lord is upon them. But Paul is pointing out that the believers in Thessalonica assuredly are not in the midst of the Day of the Lord and that the Tribulation time is NOT upon them, as they had been told by the teachers of error.

Greek authorities tell us that in the original language the word here translated "apostasy" denotes political or military revolt—"a defection." The Greek word here is the same as the Hebrew word in Jeremiah 29:32, and it means "rebellion against the Lord"—revolt consisting of sacrificing to other gods (idols).

This is the same language used by Peter when he warns against apostate teachers who deny redemption by the blood: "But there were false prophets also among the people, even as there shall be false teachers among you, who privily shall bring in damnable heresies, even denying the Lord that bought them and bring upon themselves swift destruction. And many shall follow their pernicious ways; by reason of whom the way of truth shall be evil spoken of. And through covetousness shall they with feigned words make merchandise of you: whose judgment now of a long time lingereth not, and their damnation slumbereth not" (II Pet. 2:1-3).

Galatians 5:4:—

What about Galatians 5:4? This verse tells us, "Christ is become of no effect unto you, whosoever of you are justified by the law; ye are fallen from grace." Since this verse clearly says *"fallen from grace,"* does that mean that a saved person can stumble, fall, and be lost forever? No. This Scripture has no argument for either side of the controversial subject we are discussing. This is the only place in the Word of God where the term "fallen from grace" is used, and the whole context of the passage indicates that Paul was not speaking of falling from salvation, but *falling AWAY FROM grace.*

The teachers of legalism and Judaism had followed Paul into Galatia and were teaching where he had taught. They insisted that the Gentiles must submit to the Jewish rite of circumcision according to the Law of Moses in order to be saved. Paul opposed this teaching and boldly declared, "If you Galatians submit to circumcision after the Law of Moses, you become debtor to keep the whole law. Furthermore, you are then under the curse and condemnation of the law, and Christ can profit you nothing. If you turn to circumcision as a part of salvation, you are then *under* the law and debtor to *the whole law."*

Paul preached, "You cannot be saved by *law AND grace.* There can be no mixture of the two. Salvation must be all of grace, or it is not of grace at all. If you look to the law for justification, you miss the grace of God and the liberty it brings. If you turn to circumcision as a part of your salvation, then Christ becomes of no effect to you."

But what is the meaning of the expression,

"fallen from grace"? There are some denominations—and tens of thousands of church members
and preachers—who teach that one who has been
truly born again, washed in the blood and saved
by the grace of God, can fall from grace, lose his
salvation, and spend eternity in hell. The advocates of such doctrine declare that when a Christian
ceases to work for Christ and live *the testimony of
grace,* that person has *fallen FROM grace.*

However, in this passage in Galatians, Paul is
not discussing the doctrine of falling from grace—
or "once saved, always saved," as some refer to
eternal life. Here, the truth is that Paul is attempting to get the Galatians to understand that
law and grace do not mix. He said to them,
"Whosoever of you are *justified by the LAW,* ye
are fallen from grace." He was speaking to those
who sought justification through works instead of
by faith. Evidently there were some in the Ga-
latian church who thought they were not saved *by
grace alone,* but that they must add some of the
works of the law. To refute such error Paul wrote
the marvelous words contained in Galatians 5:4.

Luke 9:62:—

Now let us look briefly at Luke 9:62, which
reads, "Jesus said unto him, No man, having put
his hand to the plough, and looking back, is fit
for the Kingdom of God." Does this mean that
it is possible to start with Christ—and then turn

back and not be fit for heaven? No, I do not see
that interpretation of this Scripture. This particular verse was our Lord's answer to a man who
volunteered to follow Him and then marred his
offer by making a request. The man said, "Lord,
I will follow thee; but let me first go bid them
farewell, which are at home at my house" (v. 61).

The answer Jesus gave this man shows that the
Lord knew that here was a heart not thoroughly
yielded to the service of Christ and that the man
was therefore unfit to be a true disciple. Jesus
gave an illustration of a man plowing. This was
a subject and a practice with which His listeners
were probably familiar. To put one's hand to the
plow—and then look back—would be to plow a
crooked furrow and produce a poor crop. In other
words, Jesus was teaching that it is impossible to
serve Christ with a divided heart. If we are going
to *look back* we will not be fit to be His disciples.
He must have all of our heart, all of our loyalty,
or none. In this case, the man's heart was divided
between the Lord and his family, and the con-
clusion is of a necessity that he had never fully
given himself to Christ, he had never been saved.

We should read such passages with many search-
ings of the heart. Not many are called to make
such sacrifices as leaving one's family, but often
we do find the difficulties very great if we follow
Christ with full devotion. The atmosphere of the
world is still very unfavorable to Christianity.

There is still need for thorough, unflinching, un-compromising and whole-hearted decision in fol-lowing Him. Our straight-forward decisions for Christ may cost us something for the present, but great will be our reward in eternity.

I have often been told—and I imagine you have heard the same comment—that *man is a free moral agent,* therefore if he chooses to forsake Christ it is his own personal affair; that man has a will and a right to do as he pleases in this matter. *I find no such doctrine in the Bible!* It is true that man is a free moral agent insofar as he has the right to choose or reject Christ as he wills; but *once he ACCEPTS Christ,* he then belongs to God and is no longer free to do as he pleases. "What? know ye not that your body is the temple of the Holy Ghost which is in you, which ye have of God, and *ye are not your own? For ye are BOUGHT WITH A PRICE:* therefore glorify God in your body, and in your spirit, which are God's" (I Cor. 6:19, 20).

By accepting Christ as Saviour, man admits that he cannot, of himself and by his own good works, satisfy the holy demands of a holy God. It is then that he ceases to be his own and belongs to God. The floodgates of grace are opened, grace becomes sovereign and reigns unto eternal life (Rom. 5:21).

Unconfessed Sins

Many people are concerned about what happens

if a Christian dies with unconfessed sin in his life. Personally, I doubt that many Christians have died without at least *some* unconfessed sin in their lives, because no matter how dedicated the heart may be, *no one* can live *a perfect life.* God's Word tells us that *"to him that KNOWETH TO DO GOOD, and DOETH IT NOT, to him it is SIN"* (James 4:17). We read also that *"whatsoever is NOT OF FAITH is SIN"* (Rom. 14:23). Jesus Christ is the only One who ever lived an absolutely sinless life. In this mortal body of imperfect flesh there are sins of which we are often unaware. I have always been thankful for I John 1:9: "If we confess our sins, He is faithful and just to forgive us our sins, and to cleanse us from all unrighteousness." (This precious promise does not say "If we *name* our sins and confess them.") However, at the judgment seat of Christ (which will be for believers only) all such matters will be taken care of and the believer's failures will never be referred to again for all eternity.

A question (usually hypothetical) often asked is, "If a man professes to be saved and then goes back to the liquor bottle and dies drunk, will he be saved or lost?" In the first place, it is not for us to judge such things. It is not for us to pronounce people to heaven or to hell. "Who shall lay anything to the charge of God's elect? It is God that justifieth" (Rom. 8:33). ". . . judge nothing before the time" (I Cor. 4:5). I cannot judge, but I can give Bible facts; and it is a fact that God's Word declares that no drunkard shall enter into the Kingdom of God. In I Corinthians 6:10 we read, "Nor thieves, nor covetous, *nor drunkards,* nor revilers, nor extortioners, *shall inherit the Kingdom of God."* Therefore, by and upon that plain statement we must conclude that a *drunkard* is not saved. I believe it is possible for a Christian to yield to temptation and *drink,* but on the basis of God's Word I do not believe he will die a drunkard.

Another Bible fact is that if a Christian continues in known and unconfessed sin he will not live long. He will commit the "sin unto death" (I Cor. 11:30-32; I John 5:16). Upon this plain Bible truth we can safely conclude that a man who lives and prospers in sin has never been saved.

If you had loved ones who died drunk or in sin, do not try to figure out their eternal destiny. Leave the matter in the hands of God, the One who judges all men righteously. Your main concern now is with the living. Try to lead them to Christ. Help the weak brethren to grow stronger. Hold up the hands of the feeble ones. And keep before you at all times the fact that although God is loving and merciful, He never condones sin. Also bear in mind that not all who profess to be saved are really saved. If you are a born again believer it is your solemn duty, as well as your privilege, to help those around you to make their calling and election sure (II Pet. 1:10)—something that will count for eternity.

The Sin unto Death

"If any man see his brother sin a sin which is not unto death, he shall ask, and he shall give him life for them that sin not unto death. *There is a sin unto death.* I do not say that he shall pray for it. All unrighteousness is sin: and there is a sin not unto death. We know that whosoever is born of God sinneth not; but he that is begotten of God keepeth himself, and that wicked one toucheth him not. And we know that we are of God, and the whole world lieth in wickedness. And we know that the Son of God is come, and hath given us an understanding, that we may know Him that is true, and we are in Him that is true, even in His Son Jesus Christ. This is the true God, and eternal life. Little children, keep yourselves from idols. Amen" (I John 5:16-21).

Ignorance of the scriptural teaching concerning sin has caused a lot of suffering, anxiety, fear, and loss of reward by believers. The *sin of UNBELIEF* is the sin that damns the soul (John 3:18; 16:9). Every soul that goes to hell goes because of the sin of unbelief—in other words, failure to believe on the Lord Jesus Christ as Saviour. There are sins that rob the *believer* of victory, joy and reward

(I Cor. 3:11-15), but there is also a sin that robs the believer of *physical*—not spiritual—*LIFE*. We will see what the Scripture reveals to us concerning this sin. Let us study our opening verse from John's first Epistle, step by step:

"If any man see his brother sin a sin which is NOT UNTO DEATH," he shall pray for that brother and God will "give him life for them that sin not unto death. *There IS a sin UNTO DEATH. I do not say that he shall pray for it.*"

Notice: It is a "brother" who sees his "brother" sin, and when the Word of God speaks of "brothers" or "brethren" the reference is to *SPIRITUAL brothers* unless it is clearly stated that the account has to do with brothers *in the flesh.* Our present Scripture definitely refers to *spiritual* brothers.

If a spiritual brother sees his spiritual brother *"sin a sin which is NOT unto death...."* Since we know that "the wages of sin is death" (Rom. 6:23; James 1:15), and the sin mentioned here is said to be *"NOT unto death,"* there must be something singular about this sin. Indeed there is! The sin mentioned here has to do with sin committed by a *believer*, not the sin of an unbeliever. To the unregenerate, the unsaved person, the wages of sin IS death, but if a Christian "brother" sees another Christian brother sin a sin that is not unto death, he can *pray* for his sinning brother, and God will hear and will allow the erring brother to live.

The Sin unto Death

Please bear in mind that this speaks of *physical* life, not spiritual life. We know that one man cannot pray a prayer that will save the soul of another, but spiritual brothers can pray the prayer of faith that will save a believer from physical death:

"And the prayer of faith shall save the sick, and the Lord shall raise him up; and if he have committed sins, they shall be forgiven him. Confess your faults one to another, and pray one for another, that ye may be healed. The effectual fervent prayer of a righteous man availeth much" (James 5:15, 16).

"There is a SIN UNTO DEATH," and there is no point in praying for a believer who has *committed* the sin unto death. All unrighteousness is sin, all that is not right is wrong, and wrong is sin. But this sin brings actual, physical death. Sometimes a believer dies—suddenly, almost mysteriously. Perhaps it is a young person with many opportunities ahead; or a person who seems to be in a position to do much good. When such a believer is suddenly taken out, removed from the living, we are prone to ask, *"Why?"* We may say, "He (or *she*, as the case may be) was such a wonderful person, he (or she) was doing so much good and was so badly needed." In our finite understanding we feel it to be great tragedy for that particular believer to be suddenly taken out of this world where the need for active Christians

is so great. But we must remember that man cannot see into the future, he thinks primarily of the present, and he looks only on the outward appearance. *God* knows *all* of the tomorrows— yea, even unto the endless ages of the eternity that follows time—and He looks on the heart. Therefore, in His infinite wisdom, He will not allow a child of His to remain long on this earth if, by rebellion and willful disobedience, that child is bringing reproach, shame and disgrace to the name of Jesus!

Do we have Bible to prove this? If we did not, I certainly would not have made the statement. Shall we look at some instances that prove scriptural basis for "the sin UNTO DEATH"?

The Example in the Church at Corinth

In Paul's first letter to the Christians at Corinth, chapter 11, verses 17 through 34, we read this dissertation:

"Now in this that I declare unto you I praise you not, that ye come together not for the better, but for the worse. For first of all, when ye come together in the church, I hear that there be divisions among you; and I partly believe it. For there must be also heresies among you, that they which are approved may be made manifest among you. When ye come together therefore into one place, this is not to eat the Lord's supper. For in eating every one taketh before other his own supper: and one is hungry, and another is drunken. What? Have ye not houses to eat and to drink in? or despise ye the church of God, and shame them that have not? What shall I say to you? Shall I praise you in this? I praise you not.

"For I have received of the Lord that which also I delivered unto you, That the Lord Jesus the same night in which He was betrayed took bread: and when He had given thanks, He brake it, and said, Take, eat: this is my body, which is broken for you: this do in remembrance of me. After the same manner also He took the cup, when He had supped, saying, This cup is the new testament in my blood: this do ye, as oft as ye drink it, in remembrance of me. For as often as ye eat this bread, and drink this cup, ye do shew the Lord's death till He come. Wherefore whosoever shall eat this bread, and drink this cup of the Lord unworthily, shall be guilty of the body and blood of the Lord. But let a man examine himself, and so let him eat of that bread, and drink of that cup. For he that eateth and drinketh unworthily, eateth and drinketh damnation to himself, not discerning the Lord's body.

"For this cause many are weak and sickly among you, and many sleep. For if we would judge ourselves, we should not be judged. But when we are judged, we are chastened of the Lord, that we should not be condemned with the world. Wherefore, my brethren, when ye come together

to eat, tarry one for another. And if any man hunger, let him eat at home; that ye come not together unto condemnation. And the rest will I set in order when I come" (I Cor. 11:17-34).

First of all, let us consider to whom this epistle was addressed. Did Paul write this Corinthian letter to *believers,* or to unbelievers? Let the Word answer:

In I Corinthians 1:2-7 we see that the epistle was addressed "unto the church of God... to them that are sanctified in Christ Jesus, called to be saints, with all that in every place call upon the name of Jesus Christ our Lord...." Then Paul says, "I thank my God always on your behalf, for the grace of God which is given you by Jesus Christ; that in every thing ye are enriched by Him, in all utterance, and in all knowledge; even as the testimony of Christ was confirmed in you: so that ye come behind in no gift; waiting for the coming of our Lord Jesus Christ."

So we see that this epistle was most assuredly written to believers—members of "the church of God," sanctified people, saints, partakers of grace, coming behind in no spiritual gift, and looking for the second coming of Jesus! Even so, they were not immune from the snares of the devil and the pitfalls of hell—and neither are you, neither am I.

Then in verse 10 of this first chapter of I Corinthians Paul wrote: "Now I beseech you, BRETHREN, by the name of our Lord Jesus Christ, that ye all speak the same thing, and that there be no divisions among you; but that ye be perfectly joined together in the same mind and in the same judgment." Here the apostle addressed the Corinthians as *"brethren,"* and certainly he meant *brethren IN THE LORD* because the Corinthians were not his brothers in the flesh.

To *"beseech"* means "to beg earnestly." Paul was pleading with these believers to behave like children of God—i. e., speak the same thing, have no divisions among themselves, be *"perfectly joined together* in the same mind and in the same judgment."

Sins of saints begin small, very small—but they grow rapidly if they are not dealt with immediately. As we study the situation at Corinth, we note that the believers there *first* began to quarrel and argue about who baptized them (I Cor. 1:11-17). This led to envy, strife, and divisions in the Corinthian assembly (I Cor. 3:1-8).

Paul asked these contentious Christians, "Know ye not that ye are the temple of God, and that the Spirit of God dwelleth in you?" And he followed that question with this solemn warning: *"If any man defile the temple of God, him shall God DESTROY;* for the temple of God is holy, *which temple ye are"* (I Cor. 3:16, 17). (The "temple" here refers to the *body,* not the soul. If God destroyed the soul for defiling the body, then salvation would be of works and not of grace, and we know this is not true. See Titus 3:5.)

While the quarreling and dissension continued over secondary matters in the Corinthian church, drawing the Corinthian believers even farther away from the primary concern of winning souls and maintaining a Christian testimony before unbelievers, one of the young men in the church took his father's wife and committed fornication with her. The astonishing—and shameful—reaction of the Corinthian believers to this situation was not one of concern for this young man's unchristian behavior, but rather, they were "puffed up" about it! In I Corinthians 5:1-5 Paul wrote to them this stern rebuke:

"It is *reported commonly* that there is fornication among you, and such fornication as is *not so much as named* among the Gentiles, that one should have his father's wife! *And ye are PUFFED UP, and have not rather MOURNED*, that he that hath done this deed might be taken away from among you. For I verily, as absent in body, but present in spirit, have judged already, as though I were present, concerning him that hath so done this deed, in the name of our Lord Jesus Christ, when ye are gathered together, and my spirit, with the power of our Lord Jesus Christ, *to deliver such an one unto Satan FOR THE DESTRUCTION OF THE FLESH, that the spirit may be saved in the day of the Lord Jesus!*"

What a sad commentary on what can happen

in a group of Christians who are divided over minor points of doctrine, such as water baptism, or, in this particular instance, over which minister of the Gospel had baptized the various members of that congregation. When we as Christians begin to major on the minor, we lose our ability to discern what is *important* in spiritual matters and as a result we become cold, careless, calloused in mind and heart.

The believers in the church at Corinth had not dealt with the case of fornication in their midst, and Paul, in rebuking them for their careless attitude, also instructed them as to what they should do about the matter. He could not be with them in person, but his written instructions were detailed and explicitly clear, as set out in the passage just quoted from chapter 5 of I Corinthians:

Notice first of all that the Corinthians were to act *in the name of the Lord Jesus Christ* and with the *power* of the Lord Jesus Christ. Then, concerning the erring believer, they were to *"deliver such an one UNTO SATAN for the DESTRUCTION OF THE FLESH."* This would seem to suggest severe physical affliction. If flesh had been indulged shamelessly, flesh must be galled and broken to pieces under the adversary's hand. It also seems clear that in the day of the Apostle Paul, men who had been specially appointed by God during the transition period actually did have such gifts as apostolic authority to deliver the offender to Satan. In I Timothy 1:20 Paul speaks of "Hymenaeus and Alexander, whom I have *delivered unto Satan,* that they may learn not to blaspheme." The number one desire of Satan is to damn every individual he possibly can; but if that individual is born again, then the adversary is ever seeking to destroy the testimony of the child of God. He does this through tempting the believer to turn aside from the right ways of the Lord and embrace the things of the flesh. The devil is a master craftsman in the art of laying snares for believers.

The Corinthian assembly was to deliver to Satan the young man guilty of fornication *"for the destruction of the FLESH."* The Greek word used here is *olethros,* which means *ruin,* not destruction or total annihilation. The word means the ruin of well-being, ruin insofar as the *purpose* of what is referred to is concerned. Such ruin and "destruction" is definitely the work of Satan, but in a case such as that under discussion here, God *permits* it as an act of judgment upon the unfaithful believer.

However, it is very clear that the destruction referred to here has nothing to do with eternal life nor with the spiritual part of the believer. Paul's instructions make it plain that the offending member of the Corinthian church was to be turned over to Satan for the destruction of the flesh, *"that the SPIRIT may be SAVED in the day of the Lord Jesus."* Jesus said to Nicodemus, "... that which is born of the Spirit is spirit" (John 3:6). Such a person as the young man described here, guilty of taking his father's wife (undoubtedly his stepmother, his father's second wife), can be turned over to Satan for the destruction of the flesh (the body), but the spirit and soul are not affected and in the resurrection such a person will have a glorified body, as will all believers. Satan is never allowed to touch the soul of a born again, blood-washed believer.

In the remaining verses of I Corinthians chapter 5, Paul makes it plain that while God judges unbelievers, those outside the church, it is the responsibility of believers in the church to deal with those of its own who live in sin and who will not confess their sins and straighten up. In verses 6 through 13 of this chapter we read:

"Your glorying is not good. Know ye not that a little leaven leaveneth the whole lump? Purge out therefore the old leaven, that ye may be a new lump, as ye are unleavened. For even Christ our Passover is sacrificed for us: Therefore let us keep the feast, not with old leaven, neither with the leaven of malice and wickedness; but with the unleavened bread of sincerity and truth.

"I wrote unto you in an epistle not to company with fornicators: yet not altogether with the fornicators of this world, or with the covetous, or extortioners, or with idolaters; for then must ye needs go out of the world. But now I have written unto you not to keep company, if any man that is called a brother be a fornicator, or covetous, or an idolater, or a railer, or a drunkard, or an extortioner; with such an one no not to eat. For what have I to do to judge them also that are without? Do not ye judge them that are within? But them that are without *God* judgeth. Therefore put away from among yourselves that wicked person."

Anyone who will receive the Word of God must admit the truth set forth here. This man who was a member of the church at Corinth took up with his father's wife, committed fornication with her, and would not give her up and repent of his sin. Because of the rebellious attitude of the young man, Paul instructed the church to have a meeting and turn the offender over to the devil for the destruction of his flesh; but it is clearly set forth that his *spirit* would be *saved* in the day of the Lord Jesus—that is, the period immediately after the Rapture of the Church. *This is the SIN UNTO DEATH.* The Corinthians did not meet as a church to ask God to forgive this young man's sin of fornication, nor to ask God to spare him. They met for the purpose of committing him to the devil for the destruction of his flesh—i. e., the death of his body.

This experience, however, did not sufficiently awaken the Corinthian believers to the seriousness of their careless attitude toward Christian conduct.

The Sin unto Death

If you will read on into the chapters that follow in this, Paul's first epistle to the Corinthian church, you will note that the apostle continues in the same serious rebuke, urging these believers to realize their full obligation as Christians. They continued to quarrel about various things. They went to law with each other about matters which should have been settled at the altar in the church instead of in Civil Courts before civil authorities (I Cor. 6:1-8). They argued about the right-or-wrong of eating meats, especially meats that had been offered to idols (I Cor. 8:1-13), and they misbehaved at the Lord's table to the extent of making gluttons of themselves. They did not eat their regular meal at home before coming to the church, eating like gluttons at the Lord's table and drinking wine until they were drunk! In this, some of them had committed the sin unto death, as Paul plainly told them in I Corinthians 11:17-34. He said: "For this cause many are weak and sickly among you, *and many SLEEP* (are dead)" (verse 30).

Now notice carefully verses 31 and 32 of I Corinthians 11: "For if we would judge ourselves, we should not be judged. But when we are judged, we are chastened of the Lord, that we should not be condemned with the world."

"If we would JUDGE OURSELVES...." That is, if we would see our sins, confess to God and ask Him to forgive our sins, "He is faithful and

just to forgive us our sins, and to cleanse us from all unrighteousness" (I John 1:9).

"*. . . we should not be judged.*" If we would judge ourselves and confess our sins, God would not be compelled to judge us; but if we do not recognize sin in our life, confess it and forsake it, then God has no alternative but to judge us.

"*But when we are judged, we are CHASTENED of the Lord . . . .*" By unconfessed sin we force God to judge us because He is our Father, we are His children, and because He loves us He chastens us. In Hebrews 12:6-8 we read: "For *whom the Lord loveth He chasteneth,* and scourgeth every son whom He receiveth. If ye endure chastening, God dealeth with you as with *sons;* for what son is he whom the father chasteneth not? But *if ye be WITHOUT CHASTISEMENT, whereof all are partakers, then are ye bastards, and not sons.*" God judges His children when we fail to judge ourselves, He chastens us because He loves us, and He does not want us to be "*condemned with the WORLD.*"

I must confess that I do not fully understand Romans 8:28, but the longer I live for the Lord and the more I see and experience, the more fully I do understand that ALL THINGS WORK TO-GETHER for good to those who love the Lord— and that means all who are born again. Whatever God permits to happen to His child (the truly born again Christian) is for the Christian's good and God's glory. FACE IT: God can get more glory out of the death of His child—that is, by removing him from this life—than He can get out of permitting a disobedient child to live a defeated life *and bring reproach on the name of Jesus and upon other believers!*

However, I would hasten to assure you that not all sickness, as having to do with believers, is because of sin in the lives of those individuals. Nor is all premature or tragic death among believers due to the commission of the sin unto death. Sometimes, through seeming tragedy in the life of a Christian, God speaks to others—to some member of the family, to a close friend, to someone with whom that particular Christian is associated. God's thoughts are not our thoughts, His ways are not our ways. "For as the heavens are higher than the earth," so are His ways higher than our ways, and His thoughts than our thoughts (Isa. 55:8, 9).

You may rest assured that *God is RIGHT* in whatever He does or whatever He allows. *God cannot do wrong.* I am convinced that some of the dearest, most spiritual children of God are sick, perhaps in wheelchairs or on hospital beds, not because of personal sins, but to God's glory. All born again believers are members of the same body, the body of Christ, baptized into that body by the Holy Spirit: "For as the body is one, and hath many members, and all the members of that one body, being many, are *ONE BODY: so also is Christ.* For by one Spirit are we all baptized into one body, whether we be Jews or Gentiles, whether we be bond or free; and have been all made to drink into one Spirit. For the body is not one member, but many" (I Cor. 12:12-14). Ephesians 5:30 declares, "For we are members of His (Christ's) body, of His flesh, and of His bones." Therefore, since we are all members of one body we are all members one of another, and in God's infinite love and wisdom He works out His own will for our good and His glory. We have no right to question His doings.

God our Father and Jesus our Saviour are a hundred thousand times more concerned about our success as believers than we ourselves are concerned, *and nothing—I mean NOT ONE THING—* can happen to a believer without God's permission. *BUT KNOW THIS:* All that God *has* done, *is doing,* or *ever will do* for us is *for Jesus' sake!* Notice how clearly this fact is set forth in the Word:

Ephesians 4:32: "Be ye kind one to another, tenderhearted, forgiving one another, *even as God FOR CHRIST'S SAKE hath forgiven you.*"

I John 2:12: "I write unto you, little children (spiritually speaking), because *your sins are forgiven you FOR HIS NAME'S SAKE.*"

Psalm 23:3: "He restoreth my soul: *He leadeth me in the paths of righteousness FOR HIS NAME'S SAKE.*"

The Sin unto Death

Another Clear Case of the Sin unto Death

There are accounts in the Old Testament of men who committed the sin unto death. One such instance stands out so clearly I would like for us to study it briefly. *MOSES is the man.*

Exodus chapter 3 records the call of Moses as God spoke to him from the burning bush, revealing Himself as *the Great I AM* and commissioning Moses to lead the children of Israel out of Egyptian bondage. Time and space will not permit the giving of the entire text here, but if you will read Exodus chapters 3 and 4 you will see how Moses at first objected to answering God's call, made various excuses—all of which God refused to accept—and eventually Moses answered the call, accepted God's commission, and returned to Egypt (from whence he had fled for his life many years before). (Please read Exodus 2:11-20.)

It is a familiar story, how Moses, under God's direction, led the children of Israel forth from Egypt into the wilderness, toward the Promised Land, a land flowing with milk and honey. Then, on one occasion, there was no water for the people and they turned on Moses until he cried unto the Lord, saying, "What shall I do unto this people? They be almost ready to stone me!" (Ex. 17:4).

God answered Moses and told him what to do: "And the Lord said unto Moses, Go on before the people, and take with thee of the elders of Israel;

and thy rod, wherewith thou smotest the river, take in thine hand, and go. Behold, I will stand before thee there upon the rock in Horeb; *and thou shalt smite the rock,* and there shall come water out of it, that the people may drink. And Moses did so in the sight of the elders of Israel" (Ex. 17:5, 6).

So far, so good — BUT — about twenty years later, years of wandering and hardship, the people of Israel were again without water and they rose up against Moses and Aaron, saying: "Would God that we had died when our brethren died before the Lord! And why have ye brought up the congregation of the Lord into this wilderness, that we and our cattle should die there? And wherefore have ye made us to come up out of Egypt, to bring us in unto this evil place? It is no place of seed, or of figs, or of vines, or of pomegranates; neither is there any water to drink" (Num. 20:2-5).

But again God spoke to Moses and told him what to do: "Take the rod, and gather thou the assembly together, thou, and Aaron thy brother, and *SPEAK ye unto the rock* before their eyes; and it shall give forth his water, and thou shalt bring forth to them water out of the rock: so thou shalt give the congregation and their beasts drink" (Num. 20:8).

Now please notice carefully: The *first* time, God told Moses to take his rod and *SMITE the rock;* but the *second* time He did not tell Moses

to strike the rock, but to *SPEAK to it.* Yet in
verse 11 of this chapter we read: "And Moses
lifted up his hand, and with his rod *he SMOTE
the rock TWICE:* and the water came out abun-
dantly, and the congregation drank, and their
beasts also."

Now, the Rock is Jesus (I Cor. 10:4), the living
water; and having been smitten once, He need not
be smitten again. Christ died *once,* to die no
more (Heb. 9:25-28; Rev. 1:18). Moses deliberately
disobeyed God, and God forbade his entering the
Promised Land:

"And the Lord spake unto Moses and Aaron,
Because ye believed me not, to sanctify me in the
eyes of the children of Israel, therefore *ye shall not
bring this congregation into the land which I have
given them*" (Num. 20:12). *Aaron* died prematurely
because of his disobedience (Num. 20:23-29), and
while God permitted *Moses* to SEE the Promised
Land, he was not permitted to *enter* it. God took
his life, and buried him in a valley in the land
of Moab:

"And Moses went up from the plains of Moab
unto the mountain of Nebo, to the top of Pisgah,
that is over against Jericho. And the Lord shewed
him all the land . . . . And the Lord said unto him,
This is the land which I sware unto Abraham, unto
Isaac, and unto Jacob, saying, I will give it unto thy
seed: I have caused thee to see it with thine eyes,
but THOU SHALT NOT GO OVER THITHER.

So Moses the servant of the Lord died there in the land of Moab, according to the word of the Lord— *and He buried him in a valley in the land of Moab, over against Beth-peor: but NO MAN KNOWETH OF HIS SEPULCHRE unto this day"* (Deut. 34:1-6 in part).

Moses was no ordinary man. He was an extraordinarily *great* man. He was God's anointed servant—but he did not get away with sin. His earthly sojourn was cut short, even though at the age of one hundred and twenty years "his eye was not dim, nor his natural force abated" (Deut. 34:7). God led him up on Mount Nebo, gently released his spirit from his body, and then God Himself buried that body in a spot known only to Him. Moses was unable to say like Paul, "I have finished my course . . ." (II Tim. 4:7).

The Word of God is clear on the subject of *the sin unto death.* A born again believer will never commit the *unpardonable* sin (blasphemy against the Holy Spirit—Matt. 12:31, 32). The *sinner* commits the unpardonable sin (which has to do with destruction of the soul); but a *believer* can commit the *sin unto death.* So if you are one who believes that born again children of God do not sin after receiving salvation, take a look at these Scriptures:

"*. . . whatsoever is not of FAITH is sin"* (Rom. 14:23).

"*. . . to him that knoweth to do good, and doeth*

102

it not, to him it is *sin*" (James 4:17). *Failing* to do what you *should* do is just as sinful as *doing* what you *should not* do.

"The *thought of foolishness* is sin..." (Prov. 24:9).

These verses were written to believers: "If we *confess our sins,* He is faithful and just to forgive us *our sins,* and to cleanse *us* from all unrighteousness. If we say that we have not sinned, we make Him a liar, and His Word is not in us. My little *children*"—notice, not "little *sinners*"—"these things write I unto you, that ye sin not. And if any man sin, we have an Advocate with the Father, Jesus Christ the righteous: and He is the propitiation for *our* sins: and not for our's only, but also for the sins of the whole world" (I John 1:9—2:2).

God does not want His children to sin; but He knows the weakness of the flesh, and in the glorious salvation He provided, He included daily cleansing from sins. But we must confess our sins, and if a child of God *fails* to confess his sins and trust in Jesus' blood for cleansing (I John 1:7), that can be the sin unto death! *Believer, you are REDEEMED.* You are a child of God *now.* You have eternal life *now.* You are traveling toward that beautiful place which the Word of God calls *heaven.* BUT—do not ever, *for one moment,* forget that you are the temple of the Holy Spirit "and ye are not your own. For ye are bought with a price (and what a price!): therefore glorify God in your body, and in your spirit, which are God's" (I Cor. 6:19, 20).

The daily prayer of the Christian should be, "O Lord, cleanse thou me from secret sins. Keep me also from presumptuous sins. Let the words of my mouth, and the meditation of my heart, be acceptable in thy sight, O Lord, my strength, and my Redeemer!" (Read Psalm 19:12-14.)